Moderne

Holy Grail of Vintage Guitars

By Ronald Lynn Wood

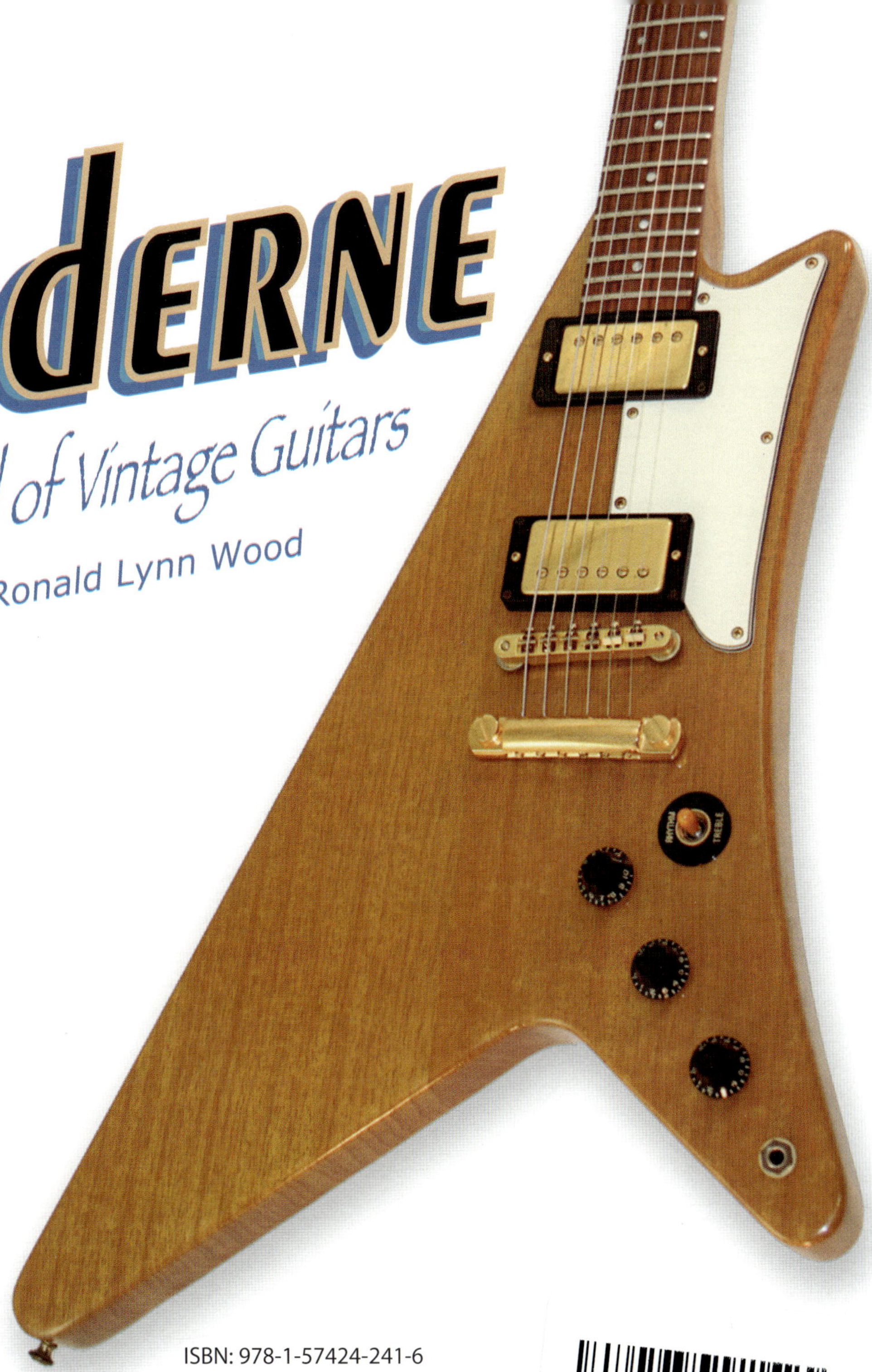

ISBN: 978-1-57424-241-6
SAN 683-8022

CENTERSTREAM

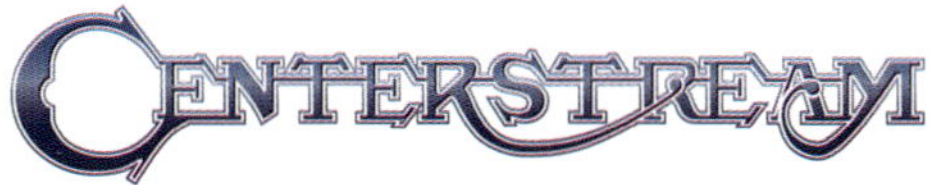

P.O. Box 17878 - Anaheim Hills, CA 92817

www.centerstream-usa.com

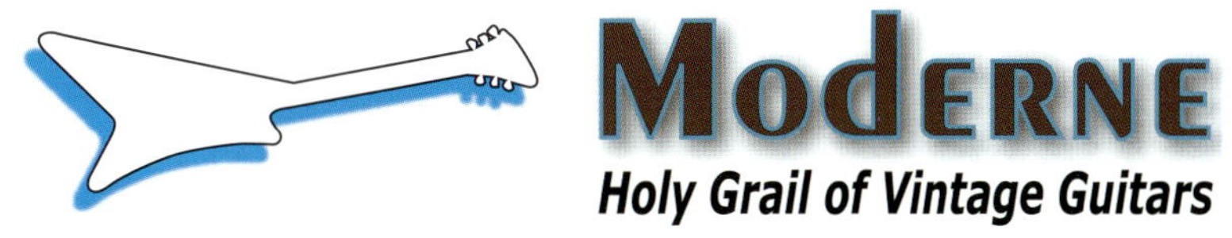

TABLE OF CONTENTS

STRINGED MUSICAL INSTRUMENT

Theodore M. McCarty, Kalamazoo, Mich., assignor to Gibson, Inc., Kalamazoo, Mich., a corporation of Michigan

Application June 20, 1957, Serial No. 46,675

Term of patent 14 years

(Cl. D56—9)

Fig. 1 is a top plan view of a stringed musical instrument, showing my new design, and

Fig. 2 is a side elevational view thereof.

The back of the article is substantially plain.

I claim:

The ornamental design for a stringed musical instrument, as shown and described.

References Cited in the file of this patent

UNITED STATES PATENTS

D. 17,888	Darbyshire	Nov. 22, 1887
D. 155,881	Evers	Nov. 8, 1949
D. 162,521	Crowle et al.	Mar. 20, 1951
D. 175,328	Van Pelt	Aug. 9, 1955
1,208,077	Ashley	Dec. 12, 1916

Acknowledgements

The Author would like to thank the following individuals for their contributions and support to make this book possible:

Mom, Dad, Rob McElyea and Laura Doty, Kerry and Karen Wood, Grandma and Grandpa, Steve Higgs, Mr. and Mrs. Olin Higgs, Billy Higgs,Travis and Michelle Jordan, Mr. and Mrs. Travis Jordan, Michelle Jones,John and Laurie Babb, Karen Hatcher, Dan Hatcher, Dane Hatcher, Danny Moore, Tim Thies, Steve Simon, Brian Waite, Jeff Johnson, Ken Steorts, Joe Rondeau, Randy Fern, Mark Farner, Robby McDaniel, Joe and Jan McDaniel, Deitz Music, Shreveport Music Company, Vince Freeman, Jim Huyck, Jeanne Berry, Randy, Bill, Dan Jones, Ace Frehley, Edward Van Halen, Brain May, Greg Howe, Heather Nova, Heather Krull, Max, Tommy Lewis and Pete Thomas-(R.I.P.), Keisha May, Dave and Cindy Buller, Geoff Ward, Al's Guitar Center, Cheryl Erickson,Greg Turner and Brenda Nissen, Pat Devitro, Donavon Hill, Lindy Frailin, Gibson Custom Memphis: Pete M, Jim H, Jim L, Jim B, Rich, Travis, John, Vince, Dave, Dennis, Audra Freeman, Heather Armstrong, Paul Reed Smith, The Saigh Family:Albert, Kathy, Sharon, Tim, Bert, Vida, Holly, Heather, Jason, Brandon, Sandip Singh, Scott Larkin, Larry Dimarzio, Rittor Music,Scott Roon, Larry Watts, Bobby Heilman,Richard Spence.

A very special thanks to:

Don Teach, A.R. Duchossoir, Bill Antel, Billy Gibbons, Bob McRann, Bob Merlis, Brad Tolinsky/Guitar World Magazine, Bruce Bolen, Chris' Guitars, Cohn Rude, Dan Erlewine, David Patrick, Dennis Chandler, Erick Coleman, Flynn Music, Frank Lucido, George Gruhn, George Manno, Tom Bradfield, Gil Hembree, Glen Miller, Greg Platzer, Ren/Heritage Guitars, Howard Leese, James Hutchins, Jim Beach, Julius Bellson, Mike Stevens, Nigel Osborne, Peter Fung, Rob Mend, Rondy Burgett, Scott Matteson, Seymore Duncan, Stan Rendell, Tom Wheeler, Tony Arambarri/NAMM, Walter Carter, Wayne Joeseph, Wilbur Fuller, Zachary Fjestad, Tony Bacon, Tim Shaw, Phil Jones, Willie G. Mosley, Dave and Tim at Dave's Guitar Shop, Chris Grimmett of Chris Guitars, Gary at Guitars West, Ron Middlebrook and everyone at Centerstream Publishing.

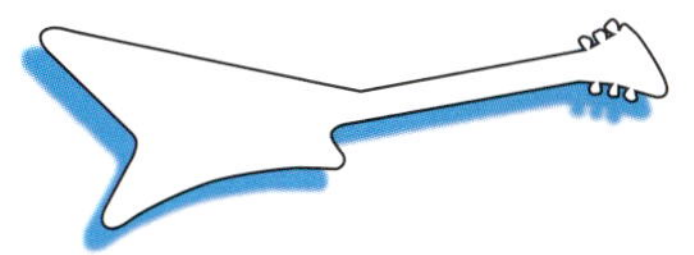

Moderne

Holy Grail of Vintage Guitars

Was a Moderne made in the late 50's? If any were built, where did they go and where are they now?

Take a trip through time to answer these questions and to discover the many facts and the many myths about this very elusive guitar.

The holy grail of vintage guitars.

The Moderne.

Chapter 1
Ted McCarty:
Moderne Inventor

Interview with Ted McCarty By Willie G. Moseley
Excerpt from Vintage Guitar Magazine
Reprinted with permission

Q: Obviously, I need to ask about those late 50's futuristic guitars, the Flying V, the Explorer, and any Moderne prototypes since they've become such collector's items.

A: I personally designed those. Fender was talking about how Gibson was a bunch of old fuddie-duddies, and when I heard that through the grapevine, I was a little peeved. So I said, Let's shake 'em up. I wanted to come up with some guitar shapes that were different from anything else.

Q: Has everything about the possible existence of Moderne prototypes been noted? If such a guitar exists, it is considered the Holy Grail of collectible guitars.

A: That's correct. We made probably four or five at the time. We had all of the new shapes on display at a road show in New York, and they did just what we thought they'd do. everybody at the show was walking around saying, "Have you seen those crazy things Gibson's got?" (chuckles). Dealers would visit our booth to look at them, and our salesmen were trying to sell them, but when it was all over and we got back to Kalamazoo and checked sales, the only thing that had really sold was the Flying V. So the question was, what about the other two? We cut 80 Flying V's in the first cutting. Dealers bought them. But I don't think they thought much of them as guitars to listen to or to play. A lot of dealers hung them in their store windows.

Q: As display props?

A: Yeah, to attract attention because they'd never seen anything like that.

A pivotal year in the history of Gibson guitars was 1949 when Theodore "Ted" McCarty was appointed vice president and general manager of the company. Holding that position for 16 years, Ted made it his mission to expand Gibson's growth and profitability. With a degree in commercial engineering, Ted and the team of engineers and designers at Gibson developed many advances in guitar functionality. One McCarty invention that was way ahead of it's time was the Les Paul. It is still produced today.

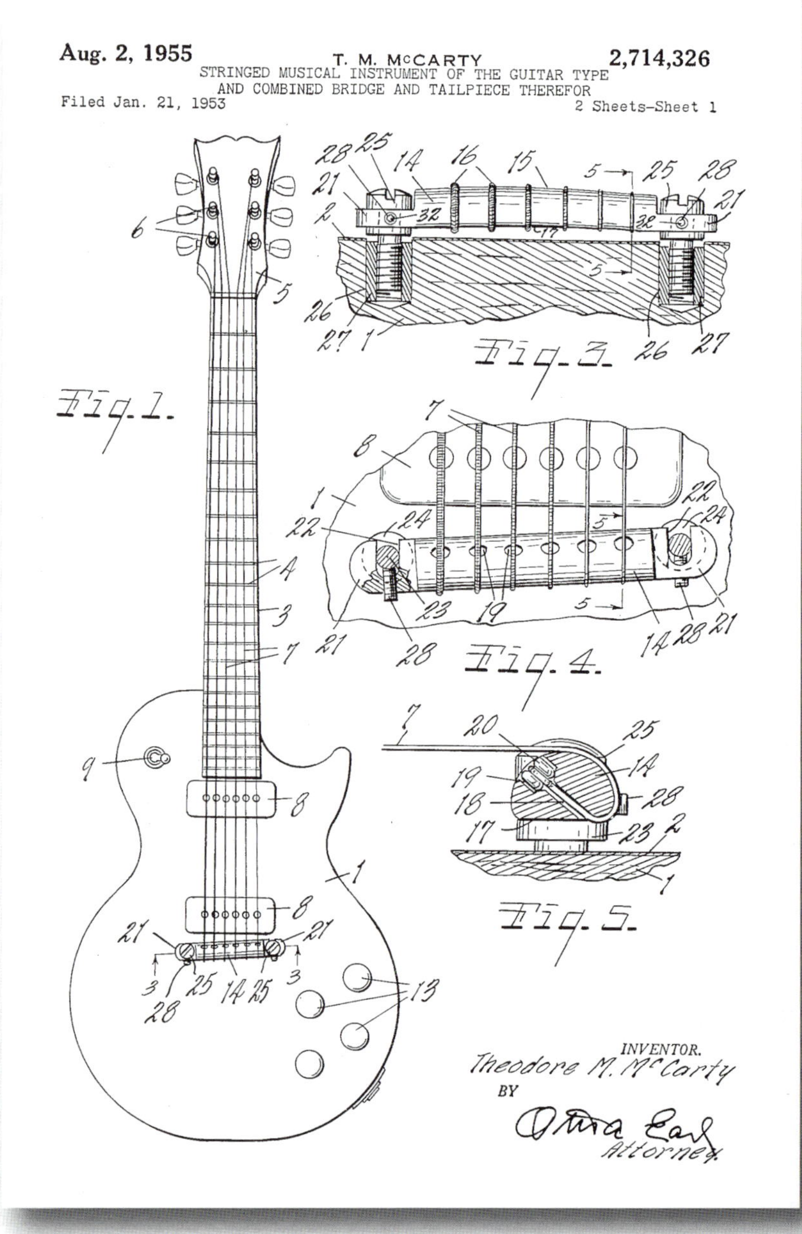

McCarty and his team developed such classic instruments as the Les Paul, Byrdland, ES-335, Flying V, Explorer, SG and Firebird electrics, the Hummingbird and Dove acoustics, as well as the Tune-o-matic, stop bar tailpiece, and the humbucking pickup.

Gibson shocked the industry when the company unveiled the Flying V, Explorer and Moderne at the 1957 NAMM (National Association of Music Merchants) trade show. While the new designs were a bit ahead of their time, the company's next solidbody, the SG, found easy acceptance. McCarty's and Gibson's best-known design is the Les Paul model. After its introduction in 1952, the model went through a variety of modifications that culminated in the classic Standard, or Sunburst, in 1958. Its maple cap on a solid mahogany body and twin-coil humbucking pickups produce a sound that is highly suitable for all rock music.

In July 1957 at the Chicago Music Industry Trade Show, a Futura prototype was displayed by Gibson. The prototype appeared to be a working model although it did not appear to have volume and tone controls.

ROGRAM

56th ANNUAL
music
industry
trade
show

ULY 15-16-17-18
1957

palmer
house
CHICAGO

Clarence Havenga, Gibson General Manager
NAMM show, July 1957

At least one other authenticated Futura prototype exists and has a natural finished mahogany body(see page 39). From the photo evidence we can safely conclude that at least one of the three Modernistic guitars existed as a working model as early as 1957.

The November 1957 issue of the Gibson Gazette, the March 1958 catalog and the April-May 1958 issue of the Gazette feature the same picture of a Flying V built with a dark colored body that may have been made out of mahogany. Compared to later production models, the sample in the catalog has unusual features such as: a protruding neck heel extending up to the 15th fret , a small contour in the lower half-wing, a side-mounted jack input placed in the bottom V cut-out, the absence of toggle switch and a smaller pickguard.

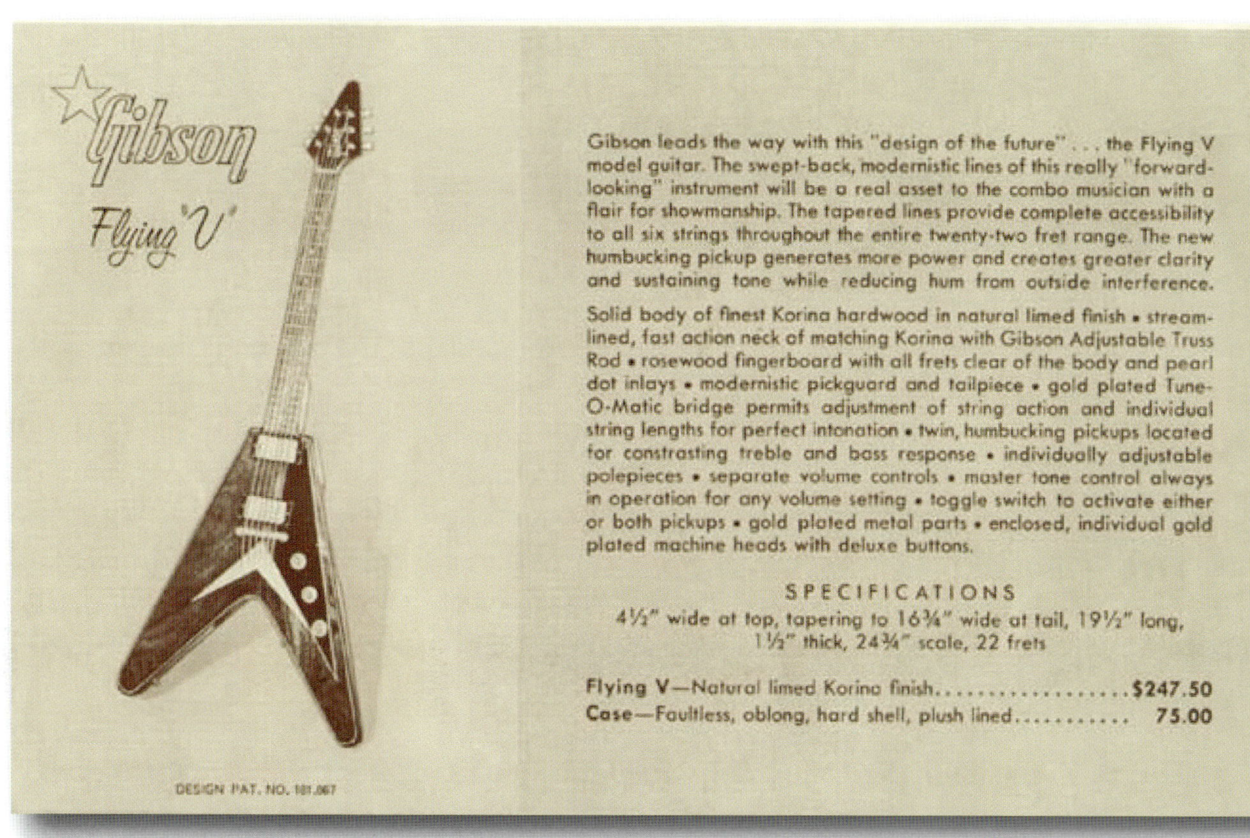

Gibson
Flying "V"

Gibson leads the way with this "design of the future" . . . the Flying V model guitar. The swept-back, modernistic lines of this really "forward-looking" instrument will be a real asset to the combo musician with a flair for showmanship. The tapered lines provide complete accessibility to all six strings throughout the entire twenty-two fret range. The new humbucking pickup generates more power and creates greater clarity and sustaining tone while reducing hum from outside interference.

Solid body of finest Korina hardwood in natural limed finish • streamlined, fast action neck of matching Korina with Gibson Adjustable Truss Rod • rosewood fingerboard with all frets clear of the body and pearl dot inlays • modernistic pickguard and tailpiece • gold plated Tune-O-Matic bridge permits adjustment of string action and individual string lengths for perfect intonation • twin, humbucking pickups located for constrasting treble and bass response • individually adjustable polepieces • separate volume controls • master tone control always in operation for any volume setting • toggle switch to activate either or both pickups • gold plated metal parts • enclosed, individual gold plated machine heads with deluxe buttons.

SPECIFICATIONS

4½" wide at top, tapering to 16¾" wide at tail, 19½" long, 1½" thick, 24¾" scale, 22 frets

Flying V—Natural limed Korina finish.................. $247.50
Case—Faultless, oblong, hard shell, plush lined........... 75.00

DESIGN PAT. NO. 181,867

Former Gibson Guitar President Ted McCarty died in April 2001 at the age of 91. He led Gibson from 1948 to 1966.

Current Gibson Chairman and CEO Henry E. Juszkiewicz said, "Ted McCarty was the architect of a Golden period in Gibson's history. During his 18-year tenure, he helped to reestablish the company's historic leadership in the industry through a number of musical innovations that still resonate today. Later in life, McCarty served as President of the Bigsby Company and also collaborated with Paul Reed Smith, whose guitar company produces several models named after McCarty.

McCarty's legacy remains in the hands of innumerable musicians worldwide and continues to inspire Gibson's master luthiers.

With a few years of producing solidbody guitars under their belt, Gibson began to get some competition from several other guitar manufacturers. Suddenly, Gibson was no longer the innovator in the solidbody guitar market and it's reputation was that of a more traditional and "old fashioned" guitar manufacturer.

The Gibson management team in the early 50s. Left to right: *Walter FULLER, Julius BELLSON, Wilbur MARKER, Ted McCARTY and John HUIS. Mr McCARTY holds an all-gold ES-175 made at Les Paul's request for a disabled guitarist.* [courtesy Gibson]

Ted McCarty became irritated by the remarks from dealers and the ever emerging younger generation of musicians who seemed to be favoring the competitors newer looking guitar models. Ted McCarty recalls: "Gibson was one of the old Jiizes of guitars, the Rolls Royce of the field. But some of the younger generations were saying, well, that's a stodgy old company, too old-fashioned, they don't have any flashy new things and so on. This irritated me and I heard it from dealers who told me this was what some of their customers were saying. The sales department would report this, same thing. So we decided, OK, we'll fix them!"

With the space race in full bloom and the emergence of rock and roll, Gibson decided to develop a new line of solid body guitars with more flashy and exciting body shapes and styles. Ted McCarty enrolled the services of artists from a firm out of Detroit where space age and the auto industry were merging. Around 1956, they got the ball rolling. Ted called in some artists and told them what he wanted and asked them to make some sketches. Sketches were brought in and critiqued. Ted called on the production men like Larry Allers and John Huis and asked: 'Can you make it?' Ted thought that although anything can be put on paper, to design it so that it can be built it into production was another matter because "you can make almost anything by hand, but production is another problem."

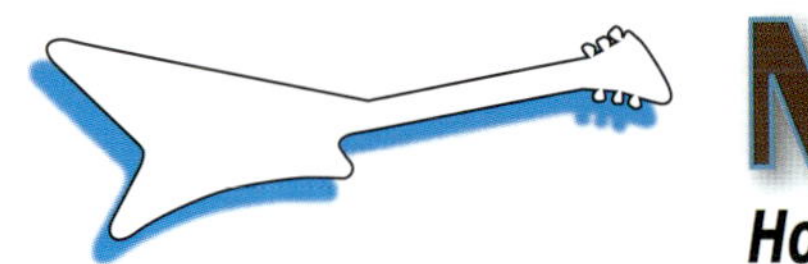

Moderne

Holy Grail of Vintage Guitars

By the mid-1950s Gibson Guitar Company had lost considerable market share to rival Fender's Telecaster and Stratocaster models. In an attempt to strike back, Gibson created three modernistic solidbody guitar concepts:the"Flying V," the"Futura" (later renamed Explorer), and the "Moderne". In the book "Gibson Guitars:Ted McCarty's Golden Era" author Gil Hembree got the official story from Ted McCarty:"Leo Fender was traveling around the country, and somebody would mention Gibson to him, and he'd say, 'Oh, that old fuddyduddy outfit. They haven't had a new idea in centuries.' Friends were always telling me about that kind of stuff," said McCarty. "The only thing that Gibson could do was come up with something way out."So I got busy and we showed the design to some of the engineers and said, 'Can we make something like this? What do you think of it?' We had a number of people who were players, like Julius Bellson, and we showed it to them. We showed it to John Huis, who would know how to make it. When Seth Lover saw it, he said (laughs), 'It looks like a Flying V'. And the name stuck."We thought, 'What can we do with this Flying V design?' Gibson was a big name a hundred years of building fine instruments and here we come out with this thing. And then we made two more guitars with unusual shapes. So we had the Explorer, the Flying V, and another one we had to name. We thought, ' Well, it's a modern guitar.' So we just called it a ModDern. And somebody came up with the name 'Explorer,' maybe somebody in CMI sales. We worked closely with sales. CMI had the finest group of salesmen in the country. In the late 1950s, those guys were making $40,000 a year on straight commission. They were good."

"We took the guitars to the trade show that January, and put them in a prominent place so people would see them. I wanted get people talking about them, saying, 'Those crazy guitars.' So I walked around to see what was going on, and I ran into some fellas saying, 'Did you see that crazy stuff down at Gibson's room?' And that went through the whole show. We actually sold maybe 40 of the Flying V. People didn't buy it because it was a guitar, they bought it to hang in their store window in New York or Chicago, to get attention and have people come into the store and say 'What is that thing?' It went into production and we made 81 of them the first year. We also did a second run of Flying V's... we just made them, we didn't bother with orders. Our salesmen were out selling, and telling people whether the models were good, bad, or indifferent. It didn't matter if they sold the Flying V.

"The Flying V was clear Limba wood; every-body used Mahogany, so the Flying V had to be something nobody ever saw before. And we wanted a wood that we wouldn't have to finish to a color. Limba wasn't used in the guitars at the time, so I got some and found out it could work very well. And it wasn't difficult to find. The people who sold the Limba called it Korina; Limba is the African name, but the people who cut it and sold it gave it the name Korina. And I don't remember if it was more expensive. We bought it because it's a pretty wood and has the same basic appearance as Mahogany, but almost white. In those days there was quite a demand for natural finishes, and Limba was the best thing we could come up with. If it was a little more expensive, you didn't care because you needed a material that would do what you wanted to do. With the Flying V, what we wanted to do was to shake 'em up. And boy, we really shook them up at that show!"

United States Patent Office

Des. 181,866
Patented Jan. 7, 1958

181.866

STRINGED MUSICAL INSTRUMENT

Theodore M. McCarty, Kalamazoo, Mich., assignor to Gibson, Inc., Kalamazoo, Mich., a corporation of Michigan

Application June 20, 1957, Serial No. 46,675

Term of patent 14 years

(Cl. D56—9)

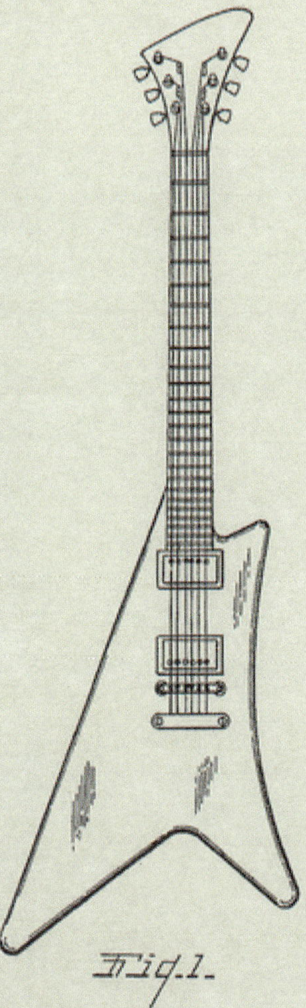

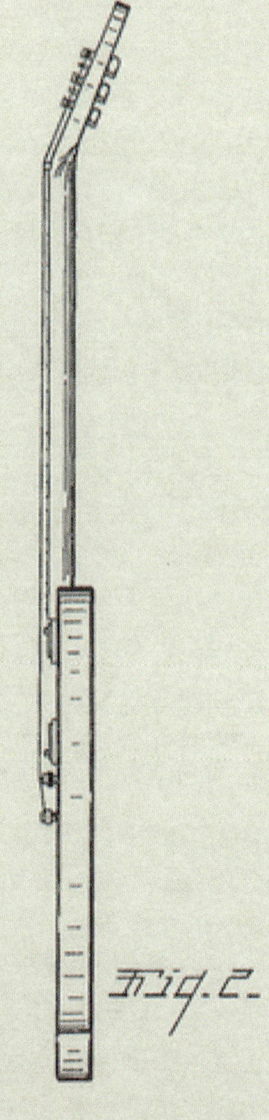

Fig. 1 is a top plan view of a stringed musical instrument, showing my new design, and

Fig. 2 is a side elevational view thereof.

The back of the article is substantially plain.

I claim:

The ornamental design for a stringed musical instrument, as shown and described.

References Cited in the file of this patent

UNITED STATES PATENTS

D. 17,888	Darbyshire	Nov. 22, 1887
D. 155,881	Evers	Nov. 8, 1949
D. 162,521	Crowle et al.	Mar. 20, 1951
D. 175,328	Van Pelt	Aug. 9, 1955
1,208,077	Ashley	Dec. 12, 1916

CMI's sales manager Clarence Havenga was looking for something new and exciting for the market and easy to produce at competitive prices. From over one hundred artist submitted designs, they narrowed it down to a few, ultimately settling on the three designs we know today as the Flying V, the Futura, and the Moderne. There are many different opinions as to the number of designs submitted to Gibson and what they might have looked like much less how many were advanced to the prototype stage. We do know that the Futura and the Flying V were made into working prototypes. Documented photo evidence of the Futura being displayed at the 1957 NAMM show exists and also a Flying V prototype was sent to the Geib case manufacturing company for a custom fitting for the guitar. In 1957, one year before the first serial numbered run of "V's in 1958, Gibson contacted Geib Case of Chicago, IL (the company contracted to produce cases for Gibson instruments from the 1920's to the 1960's) to design and tool up for cases to fit the Flying V model. As no instrument of this shape had yet been made, there was naturally no case that it would fit. Gibson sent Geib a prototype for a case sample and gave the guitar to Geib in appreciation for the work on the "V' case. As Geib was now tooled up to make cases for the Flying V, they kept the original case they made and the prototype. The owners of Geib then gave the guitar and case to a family member.

Ted McCarty commented on the Flying V: "The Flying V was strictly and wholly my idea and it was made more or less as a joke. We built one that was shaped with a round back and it was so heavy I said: 'What do we need all that stuff for, let's just cut it out!' We cut it out and it looked like an arrow. Somebody in the factory -I don't remember who- said: 'That looks like a flying vee' and that name stuck. So that's what the thing actually became."

All three of the new designs were granted patents on January 7, 1958. Interestingly, no official names for the models appear on the patents. It's possible that the Moderne was named by employees of Gibson.

Ted McCarty later commented: "For many years we never patented a model. The reason was there was Epiphone and Martin and Gretsch and Harmony and Kay and Gibson. We were all very proud, all very distinctive and nobody in that group would copy something that the other fellows made. We all belonged to the same association, we all knew each other personally and we had a personal pride. It wasn't until those guys in California got into the picture and started patenting their designs that then we began to find that if we wanted to protect ourselves, we had to go and patent ours too."

Chapter 2
The Quest
Begins

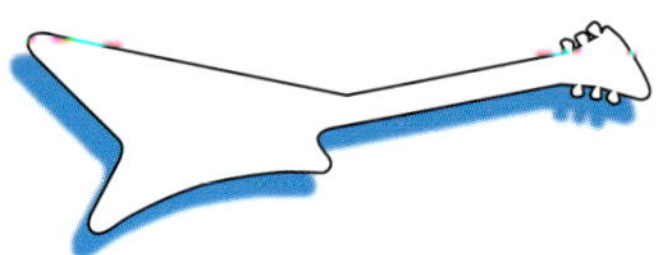

Moderne
Holy Grail of Vintage Guitars

While the Gibson Moderne has been the fascination of many guitar enthusiasts over the years, no one has seen what they believe to be an original. And rightly so. To survive the scrutiny of today's experts would be next to impossible. Even if someone had an original in their possession, the risk of it being declared unoriginal or worse, a fake, would make it the owner's best interests not to expose the guitar. Also, there are some very talented luthiers out there and forgeries of other popular models have surfaced.

Was an original made? Most people who have tried to find an original Moderne would say no. Based on my research, I might disagree. Mine is just another opinion in a sea of many. I believe its time to sort out the fact from the fiction and complete the puzzle of this rare and mysterious Gibson guitar.

The Moderne is the ultra-mysterious third design of Gibson's 1958 Modernistic series of instruments, and no one knows for sure if any original Modernes were ever really made. Eyewitness say that at least one was on display at a trade show in 1958, and it does seem likely that at least 2 or 3 prototypes would have been produced, one of them to be sent out for case fitting.

With the abundance of talented luthiers it is nearly impossible for anyone, even Gibson, to verify if a Moderne with period correct components and construction techniques is in fact real, or just a very well made copy.

It is, for many, the Holy Grail of the solid-body electric guitar world. If one were found and could be verified as a 1958 Moderne, it would most likely command a million dollars.

John Huis was the production manager during the time the Modernistic guitars were produced and said that 30 to 35 Modernes were made but that most of them just hung around in a rack for a long time. Other factory workers say that they only saw Explorers on the racks sitting for months. When Mr. Huis was interviewed in August 1993, he said: "Some were raw wood. Most of them sat there dormant. We may have put a finish on only five or six. I'm not sure about that. I don't think most of them ever left the factory."

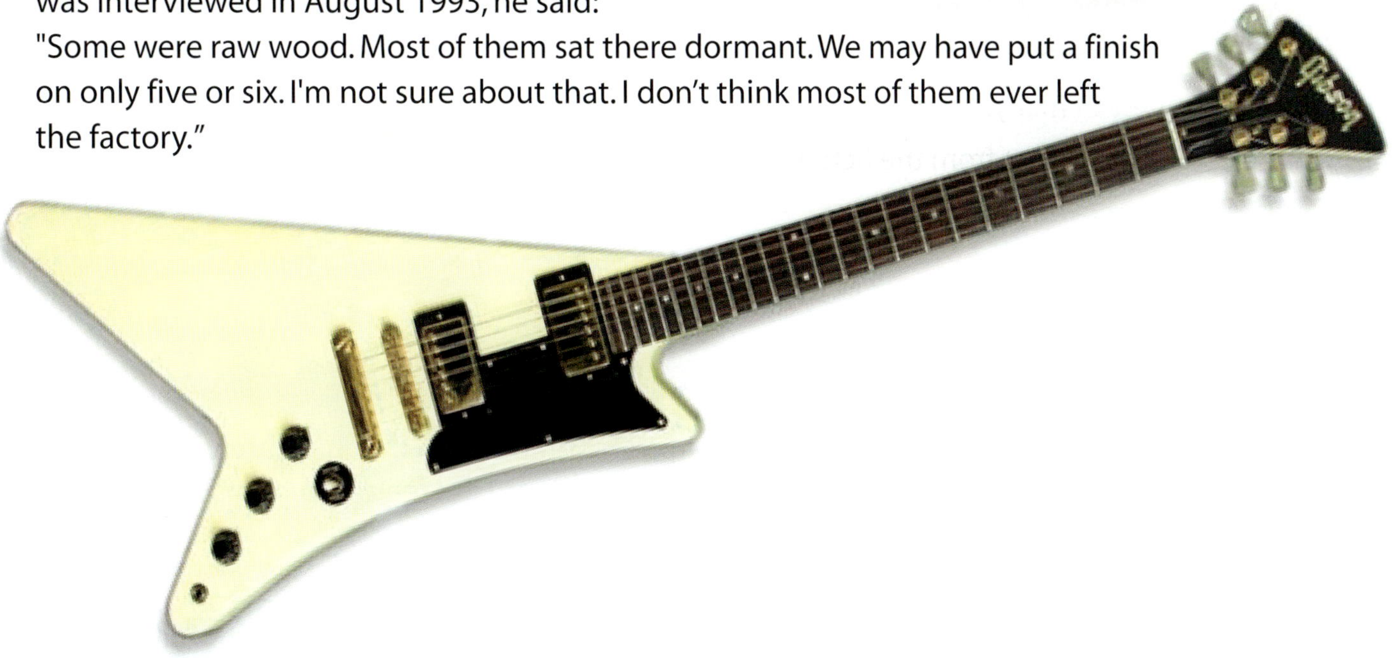

Production Supervisor John Huis(left) and humbucker inventor Seth Lover

From the photo on the right, we can see that Gibson did not cut up or otherwise destroy leftover guitars. Guitars were sometimes stripped of it's parts and the remainder shelved for later use. Employees were able to obtain rare and one of a kind guitars such as the prototype of the Futura. It was bought or given to an employee who passed it on to his daughter.

An original Futura prototype

Leftover bodies at the Gibson Kalamazoo factory.

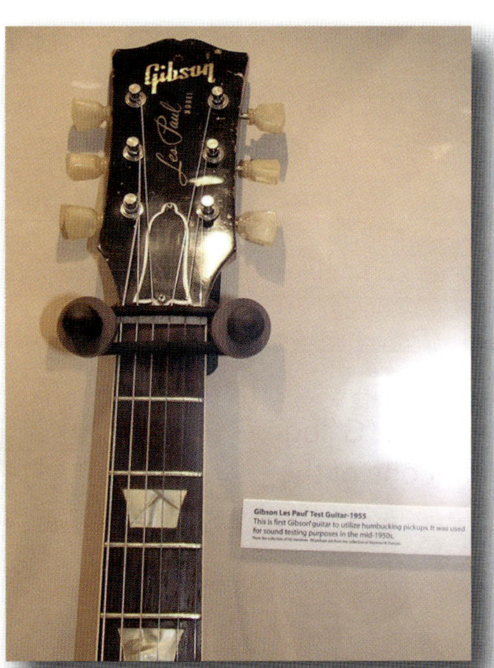

Another example of a one of a kind experimental Gibson that has survived to present day is a 1955 Les Paul which was the first Les Paul featuring humbuckers. Owner Gil Hembree acquired it from a Gibson employee's family in Kalamazoo. The guitar was hung on a wall from a nail through the hole in the headstock. The pickups are out of phase.

ES-175		A-24998	
ES-175-D		A-24999	Feb 18, 1957
ES-175	N	A-25000	H.B. Pickup starts here.
ES-175	N	A-25001	
ES-175	N	A-25002	
ES-175		A-25003	

February 18, 1957 marked the introduction of the Humbucking pickup. Since the known prototypes of the Flying V and the Futura both feature humbucking pickups, the Moderne prototype would have them as well and most likely would have been built after February 18, 1957.

Early examples of the Explorer with the split v style headstock.On the right is one with a very rare "G" logo. It is rumored that one of the original Modernes has the same style headstock.

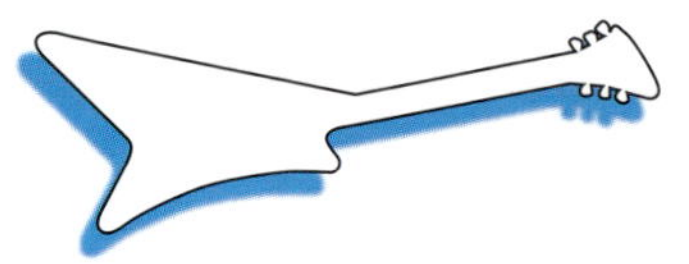

40. GIBSON, INC., Kalamazoo, Mich.: (L to R) Julius Bellson, assistant treasurer; Clarence Havenga, sales manager; and T. M. McCarty, president.

Photo ©NAMM

Photo ©NAMM

The Flying V was displayed at the 1958 Music Industry Trade Show in Chicago. Eyewitnesses report that the Explorer and the Moderne also were also displayed at this show.

Ted McCarty explained that Gibson didn't make just one of anything including experimental models. Several of each new instrument would be constructed because when Gibson would show samples, they wouldn't make just one. When making a new instrument something like the wood splitting could happen to it along the way.

When asked about the likely number of experimental samples built prior to putting only two modernistic guitars in production, Ted McCarty indicated: "Probably a dozen at the most were ever made."

Workers at the Gibson factory in Kalamazoo

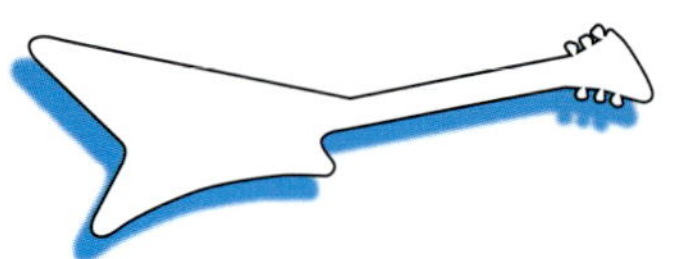

According to Gibson historian Julius Bellson, prototypes of the three designs were displayed at various conventions and clinics during 1957 to gauge sales.

When interviewed about the Moderne in the book "The Gibson", Ted McCarty recalled four models. Ted said:"We made about four copies at the most. They were made for the New York Trade Show and they were what I would call prototypes. But they didn't sell well and we never put them into production. So our sales manager, Clarence Abinger got rid of them at a cheap price to dealers".

Both Ted McCarty and Julius Bellson said there were Moderne prototypes. There is documentation of Flying V and Futura prototypes. What happened to the Moderne prototype?

There is much speculation if the Moderne was built as a prototype. If there were any finished Modernes, it seems at least one would have turned up by now. Since the general public and many music stores thought the modernistic series was a joke on Gibson's part, it's likely the Moderne was sacrificed in favor of the Flying V and Explorer models.

6 ★ GIBSON GAZETTE ★

THE FORWARD LOOK

Gibson looks to the future and finds truly inspirational design ideas. Breathtaking results of such daring are the two, new dynamic instruments pictured here. We introduce you to a new star in the Gibson line, "The Explorer," designed as companion instrument to the already famous "Flying V." The impressive appearance of either modernistic guitar would be a real asset to the combo musician with a flair for showmanship.

Engineering for both instruments is identical — they are dissimilar in shape only. Solid body is constructed of the finest Korina hardwood in natural limed finish. The extra narrow, fast action neck is of matching Korina with the Gibson Adjustable Truss Rod. Rosewood fingerboard has attractive pearl dot inlays. Tune-O-Matic bridge permits adjustment of string action and individual string lengths for perfect intonation.

The twin humbucking pickups are located for contrasting treble and bass response with separate volume controls, and master tone control. Equipped with toggle switch to activate either or both pickups. Metal parts are gold-plated, individual machine heads with deluxe buttons. 22 fret scale length.

Dealers, try one of these "new look" instruments — either is a sure-fire hit with guitarists of today!

Price: $247.50, either instrument. Case to fit: $75.00
Delivery: Flying V—30 days, Explorer—60 days

Both the Flying V and the Explorer were featured in the April-May issue of the Gibson Gazette. The Flying V may have been a Mahogany prototype due to it's unusual features that were not on the production models.

After going over the new designs, Gibson's management made decisions for the possible candidates for production models. A collaborative effort was made to build the new prototypes which would in turn be sent out via the sales department to the dealers who would in turn report back with their thoughts on those instruments. Walter Fuller recalls that the whole process was largely the result of a collective decision: "The sales force would send their thoughts and we would discuss them. It was, you might say, a family. Most of the design work was like that. It was a meeting of the minds and whether there was a need for it, whether it would sell or not and so forth."

There are also instruments in existence that Ted McCarty likes to call "mavericks". According to Ted: "There are a number of instruments on the market that I call 'mavericks'. They were instruments that we made at the factory but not the ones that went into production. Our sales managers had certain dealers around the country who were very anxious to get these instruments and they were sold to them at a slightly lower price because they were not in the catalog anywhere. In my office we had a whole line up on that wall with instruments and we'd look at them and we'd say 'No, I don't like that', so we chose the ones that we thought were the best and that's the ones that went into production." Could one of those guitars on Ted's wall have been a Moderne?

Photo©Dave's Guitar Shop

The space age influenced consumer design in the late 1950's and Gibson answered with the "modernistic" Korina Flying V, Explorer, and Moderne. Constructed of Korina, a rare African Mahogany, these guitars changed the look of rock and roll forever. Shipping records show that 81 Flying V's and under 30 Explorers were shipped during 1958-1959. As a result, these guitars are the most highly sought of any Gibson solid body.

'58 Korina Moderne

'58 Korina Flying V

'58 Korina Explorer

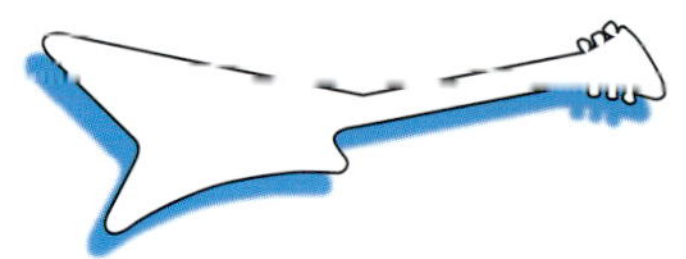

This is a mahogany Moderne with a Futura style forked headstock. The body and neck came from the Kalamazoo plant when it closed and it was finished outside of the factory(see page 194).

THE ORIGINAL KORINA TRIO

MODERNE

FLYING V

EXPLORER

MODERNISTIC GUITARS

Explorer	Guitar, Solid Body	$247.50
Flying V	Guitar, Solid Body	247.50
	Case for above models	75.00

From the July 1, 1958 Gibson price list.

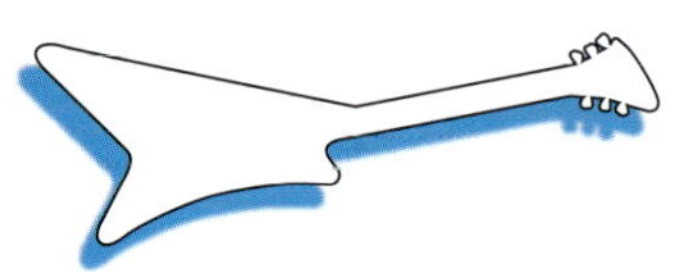

American-made. World-played.

Gibson. The first name in guitars. The final word in quality.

Two examples of this enduring excellence are the Flying V, for rock at the highest altitudes, and the Explorer, a traveller along the farthest frontiers of sound.

Like every Gibson since 1894, these instruments are created from a unique marriage of materials and expertise.

A Gibson® is mass and density crafted into brilliance and sustain. It is electronics on the edge of today's sound, destined to be tomorrow's classic.

Gibson. Made in America. Best in the world.

Gibson The first name in guitars. Yesterday, today, tomorrow.

For a poster size reprint of Gibson's U.S. guitar, send $2.50 to Gibson Literature Dept., P.O. Box 100087, Nashville, TN 37210.

An advertisement from an issue of Guitar Player magazine October of 1983.

What appointments might have an original Moderne have?

- African White Limba (trade name: Korina), or Mahogany wood
- One piece body (1 ' thick),
- One piece neck,
- 1 "A" nut width,
- Brazilian rosewood fingerboard,
- Long neck joint tenon into and past the neck pickup cavity,
- Smooth heel cap at neck joint,
- Pearl dot inlays,
- Black bell shaped truss rod cover,
- Raised plastic Gibson logo,
- Gold plated ABR 1 (Tune-O-Matic) bridge,
- Two gold plated PAF humbucker pickups with black plastic mounting rings,
- Black pickguard on early models,
- White pickguard on subsequent guitars,
- 17° headstock angle,
- Gold plated Kluson tuners (single line, single ring) with plastic tulip buttons,
- Three black bonnet knobs (two volume and one master tone control),
- 3 way toggle switch,
- Input jack with plastic surround,
- Oblong brown Faultless case.

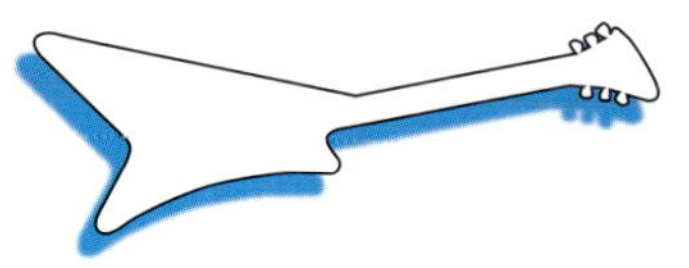

An example of the raised headstock logo. Logos from the 1950's have three prongs. Reissue raised logos have five prongs.

Gold PAF humbucker pickups with black plastic mounting rings and ABR 1 bridge

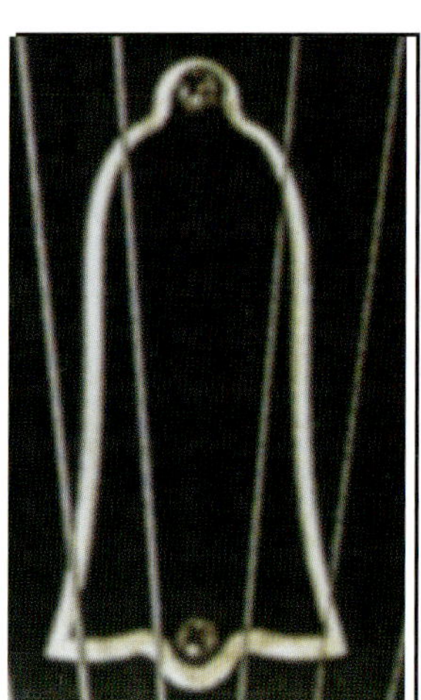

Bell Cover

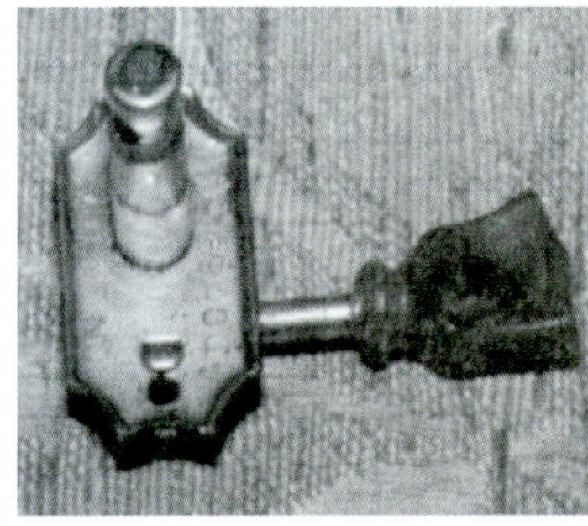

Gold plated Kluson tuners (single line, single ring) with plastic tulip buttons

Black bonnet knobs

2 ★ GIBSON GAZETTE ★

Gibson Goes to the Fair

Some of our Gibsonites are going to be part of the Kalamazoo exhibit at the Berlin Industrial Fair in Germany this month. As this issue of the Gazette is made up, President Ted McCarty, Julius Bellson, and Rem Wall of Gibson should be winging their way to Germany for the big event.

The exhibit, sponsored jointly by the United States Department of Labor and the U.S. Information Agency, puts Kalamazoo up for international inspection as an example of working and living conditions in a middle sized, middle-western American community. Gibson being an integral part of Kalamazoo industry will naturally share the spotlight with the rest of the city.

Ted McCarty will help represent Kalamazoo management at the fair — and the two other Gibsonites, Julius Bellson and Rem Wall will serve as 'live' examples of Kalamazoo workers. Both are top-flight musicians and their skill will be a part of the daily display in the Gibson section of the exhibit.

An informative article on 'Gibson at the Fair' will appear in the next issue of the Gazette — watch for it.

On their way to Berlin! From left to right: Julius Bellson, Rem Wall, and Ted McCarty, president of Gibson.

GEORGE GOBEL AT PALMER HOUSE

George Gobel, master of the tongue-in-cheek type of humor, has just completed a record breaking engagement at the Palmer House in Chicago. He played to a capacity house every night, proving beyond all doubt that he is one of America's finest comedians and entertainers. Up front with George was his spanking new Gibson L-5C in cherry red finish — the unusual color of the instrument created quite a bit of comment in the audience. This is the same instrument George has been using in his TV performances during the past several months.

Ronny Draper . . .

(Continued from page 1)

weeks, where he made his nation-wide debut.

Some of you folks out in California may have seen him at Lo Curto's Hawaiian Gardens in San Jose or in the Dixieland Jamboree and Evolution of Jazz show staged May 4, 1958 to raise money for the University of San Francisco Student Scholarship Fund.

We predict you will be hearing a lot more of Ronny Draper in the very near future. He has just signed a recording contract with Keen Records and has already waxed four sides, which should be on the market shortly. Ronny is well on his way to stardom, as his talent justly deserves.

LES AND MARY JOIN FORCES AT COLUMBIA

The unbeatable combination of Les Paul and Mary Ford is being heard around the country these days on a brand new hit record. Their first release for the Columbia label, "Put A Ring On My Finger" is a catchy number that the teenagers seem to go for in a big way. Backed up by "Fantasy," a kind of rockarhumbo tune that shows fine multi-track guitaring by Les plus fine singing by Mary.

We look for more wonderful things to come from Les and Mary on Columbia.

GIBSON MAKES THE NEWS

Gibson's ultra-modernistic instruments have provided subject material for news articles around the country in recent weeks. Quite evidently, guitarists aren't the only people who keep up with the latest thing in guitars.

The unusual shape of these new electric models fascinates people — whenever the Flying V and Explorer models are placed in a window display, that window is sure to attract a crowd of onlookers. In a satellite conscious nation the mere mention of "Flying V" or "Explorer" stirs interest—consequently the newspaper coverage.

We're naturally quite proud of this wide-spread publicity for Gibson and would like to see more of it. It's wonderful to see Gibson instruments spread across the picture pages of some big newspaper daily. Perhaps your local paper would be interested in running an article of this type, if you supplied the necessary information.

MUSIC, resembles Poetry, in each
Are nameless graces which no methods teach
And which a master hand alone may reach.

ALEXANDER POPE

★ GIBSON GAZETTE ★ 3

New Guitar Material Available

HARRY RESER, eminent artist and author, has two new books available for the Spanish guitar — The Harry Reser Guitar Method at $1.50, and Encore Hit-Kit, Volume I, selling at $1.00 retail.

Mr. Reser's guitar method demonstrates a somewhat different approach to teaching the guitar, and contains an abundance of material, including 20 lessons and 34 songs. The Encore Hit-Kit is a good supplement for this method material, and it also contains a fine selection of standard songs. The teacher will find this material valuable for use with all age groups. Both books are published by Remick Music Corp., 619 West 54th Street, New York 19, New York.

EDDIE ALKIRE, another well-known author and guitarist, has a new study on "How To Play The Guitar." The first two parts are now available, each one consisting of eight separate lessons. These solos and studies represent a new, original approach. There is enough exercise material and songs to keep both the student and teacher interested. Published by Eddie Alkire Publications, Easton, Pennsylvania. Write for complete details.

Harry Reser, with his Gibson banjo. Harry has a new Columbia LP done in the "Roaring Twenties" style—due for release soon.

DEALER DOIN'S

The big selling season is here. Summer vacations, Music Convention, and hot sizzling days are all in the past and, quite suddenly, fall is upon us. It might be somewhat of a shock to our system, but all in all, kind of a relief to get back in the regular swing of the workaday world.

The cooler days bring renewed vim and vigor to everyone and we hope this fall finds our Gibson dealers filled with this new vitality—in terms of increased sales. A surprisingly small amount of effort can result in new customers and profit for any dealer. Gibson is known as the best guitar line and sells more easily — the guitarist who wants the finest instrument in a respective price range will buy a Gibson, whether he spends $60.00 or $600.00.

✦ ✦ ✦

Enough of the heart-to-heart stuff — let's talk about what has been happening with our Gibson dealers these past few months. First and foremost, the N.A.M.M. convention held in Chicago. We were very happy to see so many, many of our dealers took time out for the show — it was wonderful to see all of you in person.

✦ ✦ ✦

Herman School of Music, Buffalo, New York recently announced the opening of their new ultra-modern quarters. The beautiful building is located at 4510 North Bailey in that city and offers the finest in facilities — both for students taking lessons there and the store's customers. Display rooms are located through the center of the building with studios lining both sides. The result is very effective to the eye and quite efficient in operation.

✦ ✦ ✦

George Gobel's appearance at the Palmer House in Chicago provided Lyon and Healy with an excellent reason for a beautiful Gobel-Gibson display. The window featured instruments similar to the custom model Gibson recently completed for George—an L-5C thin special.

✦ ✦ ✦

A new location for the American Music Store of Jacksonville, Florida. Doors of the new store opened for the first time this summer with quite a celebration. In completely modernized quarters at 307 Main Street, American Music plans to give customers better service than ever before with additional facilities for doing so.

The Gibson Flying V Guitar was the talk of Richmond, California recently due to the ingenuity of the Sealise Music Center. When the futuristic guitar arrived at their store it created such excitement among employees that Mr. Weishahn, store manager, decided to use it alone in a window display. Public reaction was tremendous—never had there been such crowds around the windows of Sealise Music Center. The store was filled with inquisitive guitarists and the phone rang constantly. Two days after being placed in the window the Flying V was sold along with a GA-400 amplifier; with more orders expected. (See photo).

Launching station for the Gibson Flying V Guitar—as conceived by the Sealise Music Center in their recent window display.

✦ ✦ ✦

Some of our dealers have been getting some nice publicity for Gibson in the local dailies. Among them Strobel's Music Shop in Nashville, Tennessee, and the E. E. Forbes Piano Company in Birmingham, Alabama. Our heartiest congratulations and thanks.

✦ ✦ ✦

Piksa Guitar Studio at Byerly Brothers, Peoria, Illinois has organized a fine student guitar band. Band members take part in two studio recitals a year, and the first place trophies they have brought home from Guild Conventions attest to the high quality of instruction given at this studio. Of course most students use Gibson instruments.

★ GIBSON GAZETTE ★ 7

CONVENTION SNAPSHOTS

This is for the benefit of our dealers who didn't quite make it to the N.A.M.M. convention—a few pictures of the Gibson display rooms. Our photographer tried to catch as much of the exhibit as possible.

Amplifiers by Gibson, with a few solid body guitars on the left.

Those wonderful electric guitars, including the new Flying V.

Here's the new double neck guitar and a double cutaway electric bass on the left.

TRACKIN' DOWN the Stars

As a lazy summer turns to a busy fall, we think wistfully of our West Coast correspondent, *Tiny Timbrell*, who will continue to soak up that well-known sun in California. With a grateful bow to Tiny for his "inside dope" on Gibsons in stardom, we pass the following on to you . . .

A large quip on the busy life of *Bob Morgan*. He has paused in Hollywood long enough to accompany the Sammy Davis Jr. Show at Frank Sennes' Moulin Rouge. Then off again to Atlantic City with Sammy and back to Las Vegas while Mr. Davis returns to the Coast for his part in the Goldwyn production of 'Porgy and Bess' . . . Another real "hustler" with his guitar is *Jack Marshall*, who is writing the score and conducting for a new Hecht-Lancaster production shooting at the Universal International Studios. A wealth of talent here as evidenced in Jack's fine job on scoring and conducting 'Thunder Road,' a Robert Mitchum production. . .

Sounds like things are really poppin' in Vegas for Gibsonites lately. *Dave Porazzo* just returned from there where he tuned up for a spin with the Page Cavanaugh Quartet . . . *The Legarde Twins* (Ted and Tom) from Australia are Las Vegas bound in the very near future. They recently recorded two of their own tunes for the Bel Canto label . . . Speaking of going places, *Jimmy Dean* left for New York where he is slated for a half-hour CBS show every day starting September 15th. . .

We wouldn't tell you this except we feel sorry for our friend, *Bobby Gibbons*. He has recently been laid up for a few weeks (painful ones) with a slipped disc brought about from lifting—of all things!—an amplifier. . .

Back to recordings again—George Cates' latest effort for the Decca-Coral label features *Buddy Merrill* and his L-5 and L-5C. Buddy is a mainstay of the Lawrence Welk Orchestra . . . If you "dig" the Afro-Cuban beat, grab a listen to *Louis Bonfas'* recent album recorded on Capitol of the World label. It's called "Brazilian Guitar" and was grooved in Rio De Janeiro. . .

Using eight guitars as well as the conventional rhythm section of bass, piano and three drummers, *Bob Bain* is very busy writing and conducting the latest Yma Sumac recordings for Capitol Records . . . While we're on the subject of records, be sure to listen to the latest recording of Moonglow/Picnic by Morris Stoloff and the Columbia Pictures Orchestra featuring Gibsonite *Al Hendrickson* on an un-amplified guitar solo . . . And *Tony Rizzi* of the NBC staff is re-united with the Dave Pell Octet for an album for Capitol Records . . . "Makin' It" was "made" by fine guitar duetters *John Pisano* and *Billy Bean*. It's a Decca LP featuring these boys with strings, woodwinds, brass and rhythm.

We guess that music more than "runs" in this family! There is quite a little ensemble of musicians around the hearthfire of *Roberta Sherwood*, the famous singing star. Her three sons, Bobby, 10, Jerry, 15, and Don, 17, all play instruments at their home in Miami. Don plays a Gibson ES-175 guitar.

Appearing with the fine Buddy DeFranco group at the 'Jazz Cabaret' on weekends is *Howard Roberts* . . . The Sheraton-Town House 'Zebra Room' is the scene of some serious sessions of the *Frankie Remley* group of Jack Benny-Phil Harris fame . . . *Bud Lee* is back from Hawaii for a few months to clear up some local business, and then he and his family will go back to the islands.

Bob Morgan—ES-350, Les Paul Custom
Jack Marshall—ES-175
Dave Porazzo—ES-335T, Les Paul Custom
LeGarde Twins—SJN (Country-Western Jumbos)
Bobby Gibbons—Les Paul Custom
Bob Bain—L-5, Les Paul Regular
Al Hendrickson—Les Paul Regular, L-5
Tony Rizzi—L-5, ES-350, Les Paul Regular
Frank Remley—L-5 left handed
Bud Lee—Les Paul Custom, GA-50

Those wonderful electric guitars, including the new Flying V.

Excerpts from the 1958 Gibson Gazette. Unfortunately, the Moderne isn't even mentioned.

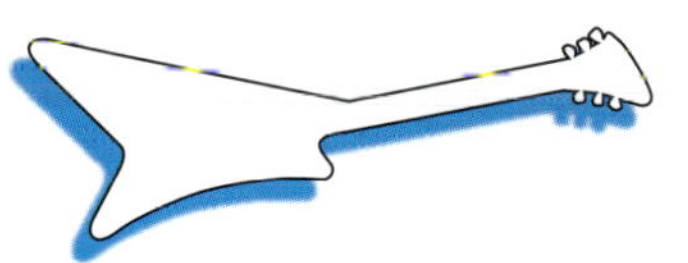

24 DOWN BEAT NAMM DAILY Chicago, July 17, 195

they've said it with

a million Gibsons

In the 90s . . . it was the Gibson MANDOLIN!

In the 20s . . . those Gibson BANJOS!

and today's favorite fret . . .

is still a Gibson!

since 1894 the finest in fretted instruments

In the years since Orville Gibson first brought to fretted instruments all the skills of the violin maker's art, more than a million Gibsons have been sold. Gibson has been *first* from the first . . . pioneering improvements for ever finer purity of tone, deeper resonance, and greater flexibility . . . developing the technique of guitar making to a fine art. Among the many Gibson "firsts" are the electric guitar, truss rod neck construction, adjustable bridge, three-quarter size instrument, carved top and back, cut-away design, and "humbuck" pick-up. Today Gibsons are heard *and preferred* 'round the world —from family room to Carnegie Hall!

Gibson, INC.
KALAMAZOO, MICHIGAN

"We Cordially Invite you to See and Hear the New Gibson Models - -
Rooms 726-7-8-9, The Palmer House, July 14-18

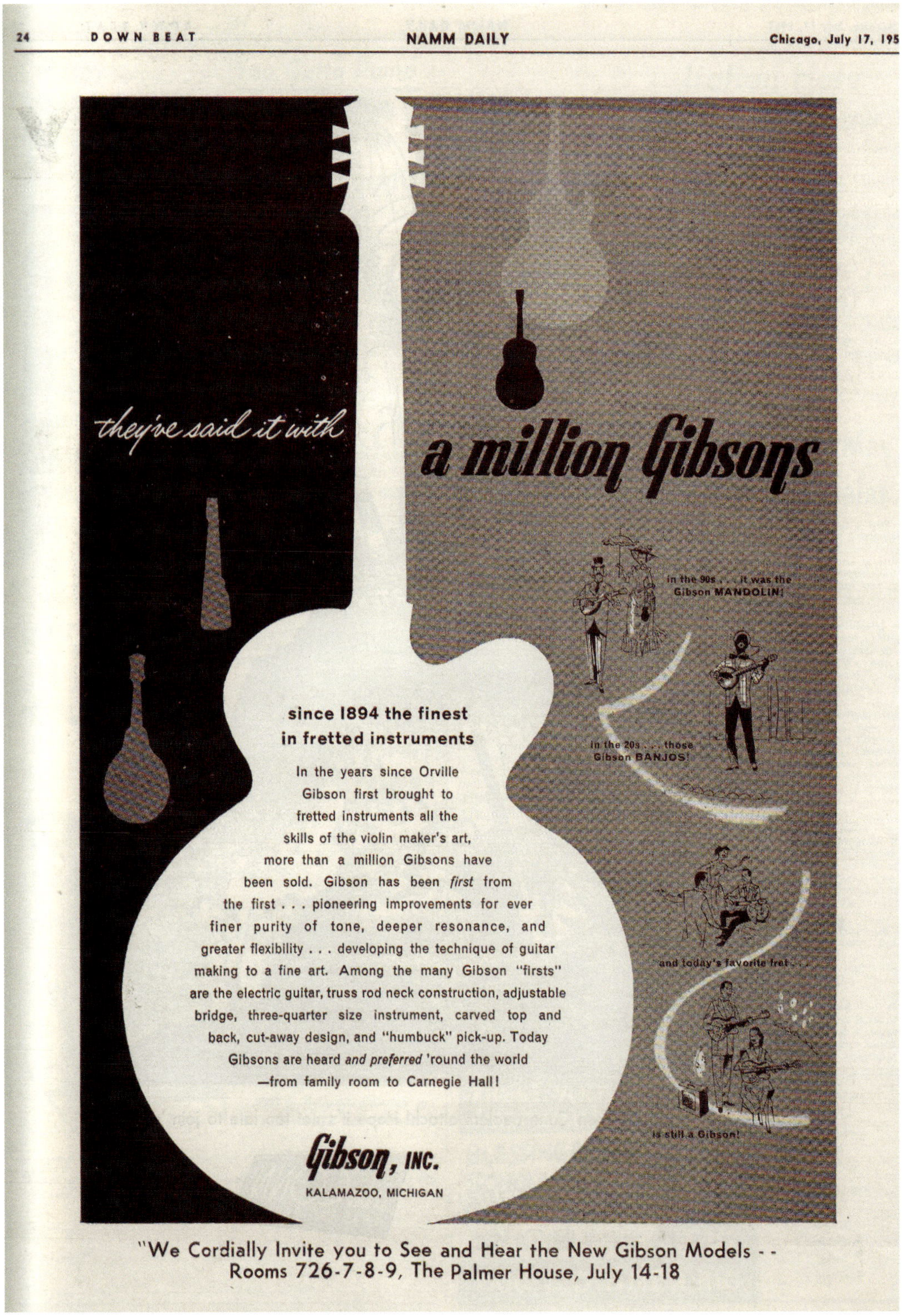

An advertisement for the 1957 NAMM show where Gibson was to debut the new "Modernistic" guitars.

1958–1959	1958	1959	Totals
Korina (Mod. Gtr)	19	3	22
Flying "V" (Korina)	81	17	98
Totals	100	20	120

The shipping records from Kalamazoo show that 19 Modernistic guitars were shipped in 1958 and 3 in 1959. There are many who think that the Korina (Mod.Gtr) guitars represent Explorers instead of Modernes yet over 30 original Explorers have been accounted for presently. The Explorer was advertised in the Gibson Gazette from 1958 with the name "Explorer" so it seems logical that it would have been listed with its intended name like the Flying V in the shipping records. That would mean that the Korina (Mod.Gtr) guitars were in fact Modernes.

Price: $247.50, either instrument. Case to fit: $75.00
Delivery: Flying V—30 days, Explorer—60 days

This is an artist drawing of the Moderne. From the drawing we see the placement of the input jack is on the inside of the lower V by the volume and tone controls. This is the earliest known evidence of the concept of the Moderne guitar.

Copy of original U.S. 2-21-93

Gruhn Guitars, Inc.

410 Broadway • Nashville, Tennessee 37203
Phone (615) 256-2033

Fine Vintage and Custom Made Fretted Instruments

Date 2/10/93

photos attached – personally examined last week
☑ I have personally inspected the instrument described below.

☐ I have examined the attached photos of the instrument described below but have not seen the instrument itself. Below is my best estimate, based on these photos, of the instrument's value; however, it is not possible to judge from photos alone the exact state of originality and need of repair, so my appraisal is only accurate insofar as the photos are representative of the actual condition of the instrument.

We certify that the guitar described below is, in our opinion, a prototype Gibson Futura forerunner of the Explorer model made in 1957

Description: No name inlay or logo. No serial number. This instrument conforms to the description of the instrument described in Tom Wheeler's book American Guitars and to the best of my ability to judge appears to be a genuine prototype. It has also been examined by Andre Duchossoir and Tom Murphy and I have discussed it with them. If we are correct in our opinion regarding its originality it should have a market value of not less than $200,000.00 (two hundred thousand dollars).

George Gruhn

A 1957 prototype of the Gibson Futura authenticated by Gruhn Guitars.

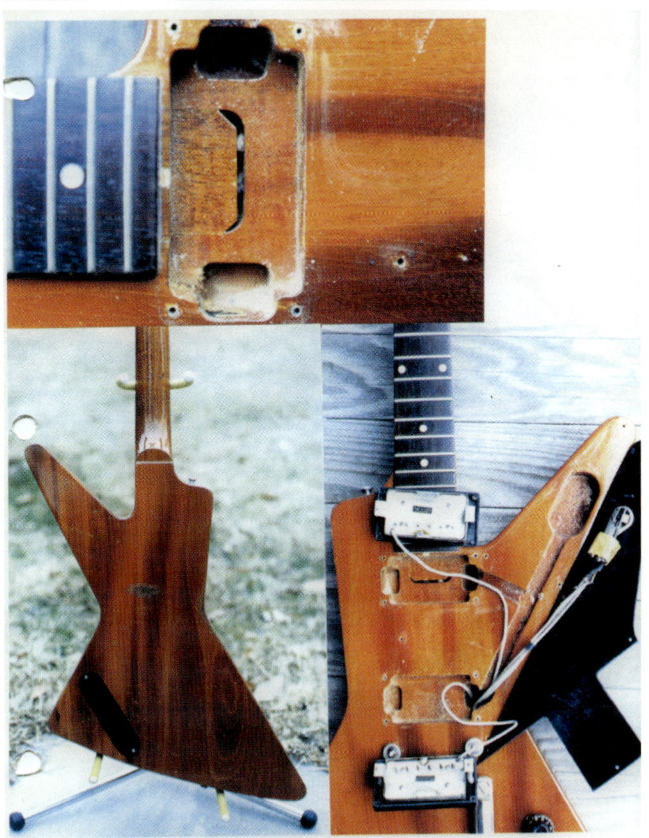

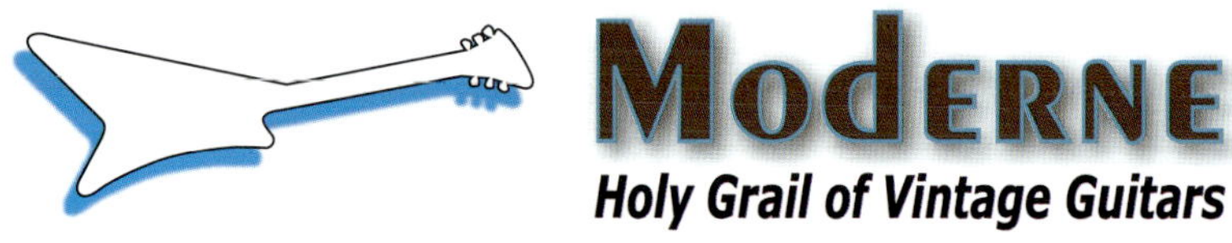

An example of a "Dumpster Dive"
This body appears to be made out of Mahogany.

When Gibson has a reject guitar, it is stripped of all its parts, then the logo is cut off the top of the headstock. The body is i cut in to two or three pieces. Years ago, you could go look in their dumpsters and retrieve various parts, bodies, and necks. Gibson now uses locked dumpsters with built in crushers to discourage this activity.

This Moderne first surfaced in the early 1970's and was thought to be original. It was at one time owned by Dan Erlewine(see pg.127).

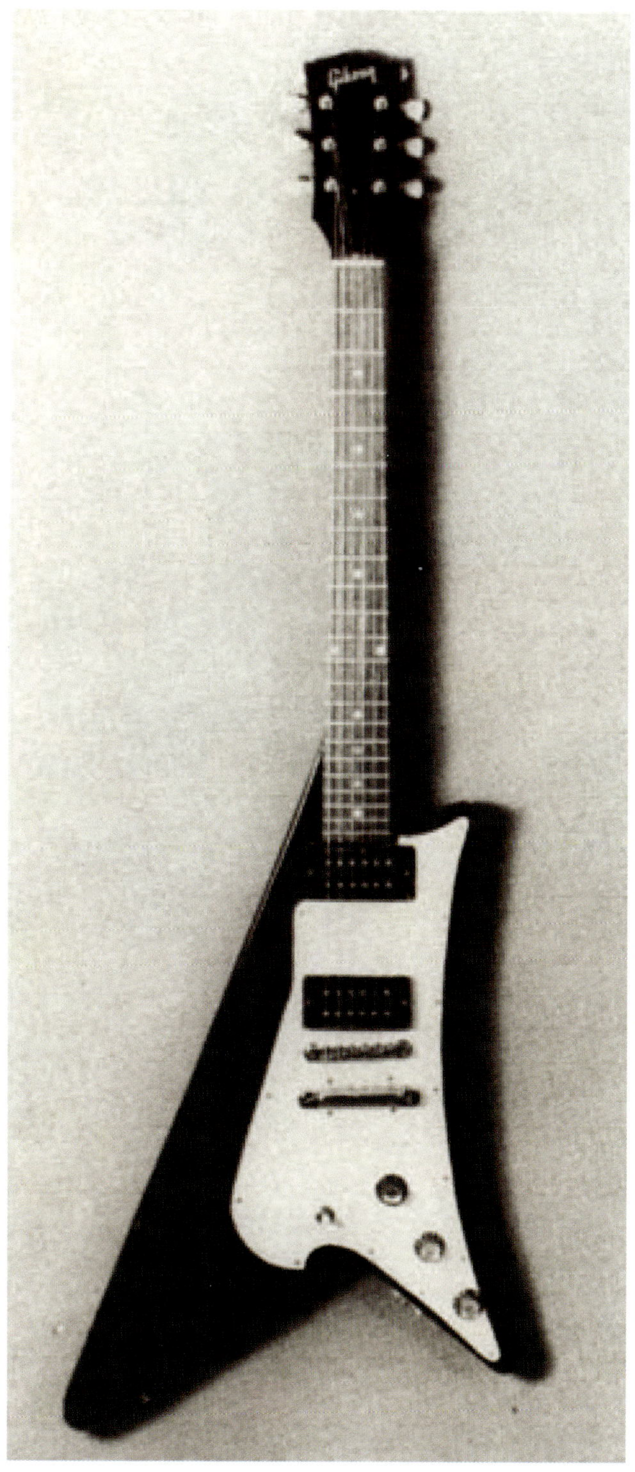

George Gruhn got to see this Moderne in person in the early 1970's and his opinion of it was told in an interview : "As for the one that was supposed to be real, an employee of mine bought it. I was excited and went out to his home at night to see it. I got there and he was outside, holding it in his hand, and in the dark I could see it was a fake. We got our money back. It was eventually sold as an original, to a Japanese collector. It's just a homemade body with a Gibson neck stuck onto it. It's laughable."

It is interesting to note the resemblance to this guitar (most notably the pickguard and the Gibson "open book" headstock shape) and the copies that companies like Ibanez, Greco, and Antoria produced in the 1970's.

Chapter 3
Gibson
Mystery Guitar

The Moderne Gibson Mystery Guitar

The mystery of the Gibson Moderne guitar can be traced back to the birth of the Rock 'n' Roll era. It's a tale that has been told and retold among serious guitar buffs for years; a story about a guitar that disappeared.

As a guitar player, you know of the Gibson Explorer and Flying V, two giants that forever changed the shape and sound of rock 'n' roll. They became legends. But, did you know that the Explorer and the Flying V had a sister guitar, designed with the others for introduction at the same time? -- a guitar the public never saw?

Because of confusion in decoding historical records, a variety of stories have been printed regarding the Moderne, each different, each claiming to be the gospel truth.

Here, as best can be deduced by current historians, is the story of the Moderne, Gibson's mystery guitar.

A new kind of "beat" music was springing up almost simultaneously all over the country. There were "hillbilly cats" in the South and "hep cats" in the North, and the younger generation throughout the nation was starting to bop to the new musical rage -- Rock 'n' Roll.

The musical impact of Rock 'n' Roll was immeasurable and it was apparent to Gibson as early as 1955 that radical innovations were called for in product design.

Selected designers collaborated with Gibson Research and Development on a mission to show these new rockers what Gibson could do. Close to one-hundred sketches and about a dozen prototypes later, three models were chosen to take to various conventions in 1957.

The issue becomes cloudy here because of a variety of names used at the time for these three "modernistic" instruments. The Explorer and Flying V were certainly two of them. As historian A. R. Duchossior said in his book, *Gibson Electrics*, "The reaction of 'professionals' towards these prototypes was at the same time one of skepticism and naturally of. . .bewilderment." What would later become two of the most influential shapes in guitar design certainly had a rocky beginning.

A single drawing of the Moderne, shown in patents submitted on June 20, 1957, is the only visual evidence of what the mystery guitar looked like. The other two patents submitted the same day? -- the Explorer and the Flying V.

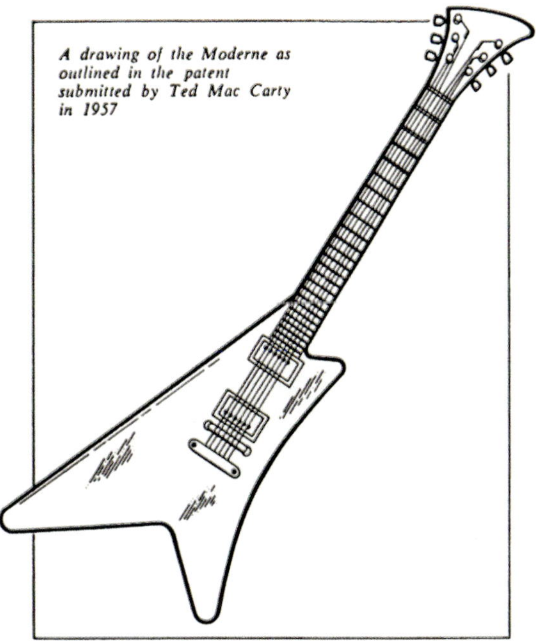

A drawing of the Moderne as outlined in the patent submitted by Ted Mac Carty in 1957

It was originally believed that 12 to 20 Modernes were produced, but a more realistic interpretation of the records would indicate only a few, probably four, were ever crafted. The prototypes were built for introduction at the 1958 NAMM Trade Show in New York City along with the Flying V and the Explorer.

However, after reviewing the instrument, Gibson administrators summized that the Modern was just too "different" for the 1958 public to accept so it never made that trip to New York.

As in all good mysteries, every clue poses another mystery and the tale of the Moderne is no exception. For example, why were so few built? Current personnel find this particularly baffling, considering that in crafting prototypes, usually close to a dozen are produced. Also what Gibson craftsman or craftsmen can be credited with designing the Moderne? This, too, seems locked away in the foggy past.

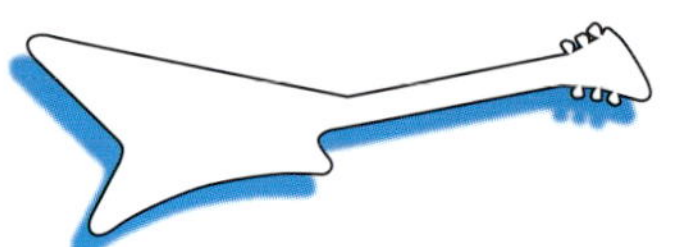

Whatever happened to those select few Modernes? Apparently nobody knows. . .nobody! Over the years there have been several claims, several clever forgeries, even rumors as to where one of those treasures might lie, "encased in the back office of a manufacturer in Japan...owned by a man in New Jersey who's "keeping it quiet".

As long as the real thing isn't found, the search and the rumors will persist, and the story of the Moderne will remain a mystery.

Three guitars. Two became legends. . .one disappeared.

Because of repeated inquiries from collectors and players, Gibson was recently persuaded to reissue the Moderne in a limited collectors series.

Searching laboriously through historical files, finding some clues here, some specifications there, Gibson was able to slowly piece the puzzle of the Moderne together, even utilizing computer age enhancement techniques to assure design authenticity.

The result is a painstakingly faithful reproduction of the original reissued in numbers so limited that each is destined to become a valuable collector's instrument.

The Moderne, Gibson's mystery guitar, lives again.

Making history.
Yesterday, Today, Tomorrow.

North and South American Offices
Gibson
P.O. Box 100087
Nashville, TN 37210

International Offices
Gibson B.V., Giessenweg 67a,
3044 AK Rotterdam,
The Netherlands

Printed in U.S.A.

71. W. T. ARMSTRONG CO., Elkhart: (L to R) Eugene Slick, of Armstrong; C. D. Woods, San Antonio Music Co., San Antonio, Tex.; and John W. Kratz, Kratz Piano Co., Akron, O.

72. ALFRED KNIGHT LTD., London, England: Mrs. W. O. Brown (left), Brown Piano Mart, Oklahoma City, and Mrs. Alfred Knight listen as Mr. Knight demonstrates the Knight Piano.

73. CHICAGO MUSICAL INSTRUMENT CO., Chicago: Clarence Havenga (left), Gibson manager, and Ted Boles, Lyon & Healy, Inc., Chicago.

74. STEINWAY & SONS, Long Island City, N. Y.: (L to R) Laurin Mueller, Redewill Music Co., Phoenix, Ariz.; George B. Williams and John H. Steinway, of Steinway & Sons; and J. E. Holtz, vice-president, San Antonio Music Co., San Antonio, Tex.

75. KRAKAUER BROS., New York: (Standing L to R) Ray Erlandson, Jr., Joske's of Texas, San Antonio, Tex.; Hugh J. Helion, factory superintendent; Guy W. Deetz, Deetz House of Music, Rockford, Ill.; A. S. Zeisler, sales manager; Gordon Early, Deetz House of Music; Albert J. Lipschultz, Uptown Piano Co., Chicago. (Seated in front) Maurice Bretzfelder, president.

76. CONN ORGAN CORP., Elkhart: (L to R) R. W. Freimuth, general retail manager, Steinway & Sons, New York; John Yousling, assistant sales manager; and Lloyd H. McCabe, manager, organ department, Steinway & Sons, New York.

77. SCHERL & ROTH, Cleveland: Max P. Pottag (left), French horn consultant to F. A. Reynolds, with Heinrich Roth, president.

78. SOHMER & CO., INC., New York: (Seated) Margaret Pope, J. D. Pope Piano Co., Searcy, Ark.; and Hank Burgard. (Standing L to R) Harold Hagemeyer; Robert H. Sohmer; Harry J. Sohmer, president; and Harry J. Sohmer, Jr.

79. SCHAFF PIANO SUPPLY CO., Chicago: (Standing L to R) Joe Kulicek, general manager; J. E. Lang, Lang's Piano Shop, South Bend, Ind.; Fred Essigg, William Dunn and Robert Simpson, Simpson & Son Piano Co., Albuquerque, N. Mex. (Seated L to R) Mrs. Simpson and Mrs. Kulicek.

80. THE FRED. GRETSCH MFG. CO., Brooklyn, N. Y.: (L to R) Bill Lanezendorf, Leland Ball, Russ Dreger and Ed Baier, all of Gretsch.

81. KOHLER & CAMPBELL, INC., Granite Falls, N. C.: (L to R) Charles Kohler White, president; Percy Haid, Pierre Music Corp., Chicago; and Charles L. Clayton, sales manager.

82. FENDER SALES INC., Santa Ana, Calif.: Radio and TV artists Roy Lanham and Speedy West (playing steel guitar), Homer (seated) and Jethro (standing with mandolin), and June Anderson, G. & M Music, Winchester, Va., playing the precision bass

From the NAMM archives we see the Futura being displayed at the 1957 Music Industry Trade Show at the Palmer House in Chicago.

Chapter 4
Prototype

The logo was conceived by Gibson's director of research and development Bruce Bolen and executed by designer C.T. Burge.

Tim Shaw, who was Gibson's design engineer at the time said that Gibson decided to brand certain prototypes with a permanent mark as to distinguish them from regular production instruments.

A metal stamp impresses it into the rear surface of the peghead between the rows of tuning pegs.

Several experimental guitars are usually fashioned before settling on final specs. Such instruments, many of which are never even finished, are not intended to be marked with the logo. Instead, the stamp will be applied only to the three or four official prototypes of each model leaving the factory for promotional purposes (such as exhibition at trade shows). These instruments are in final form virtually identical to the production guitars to follow.

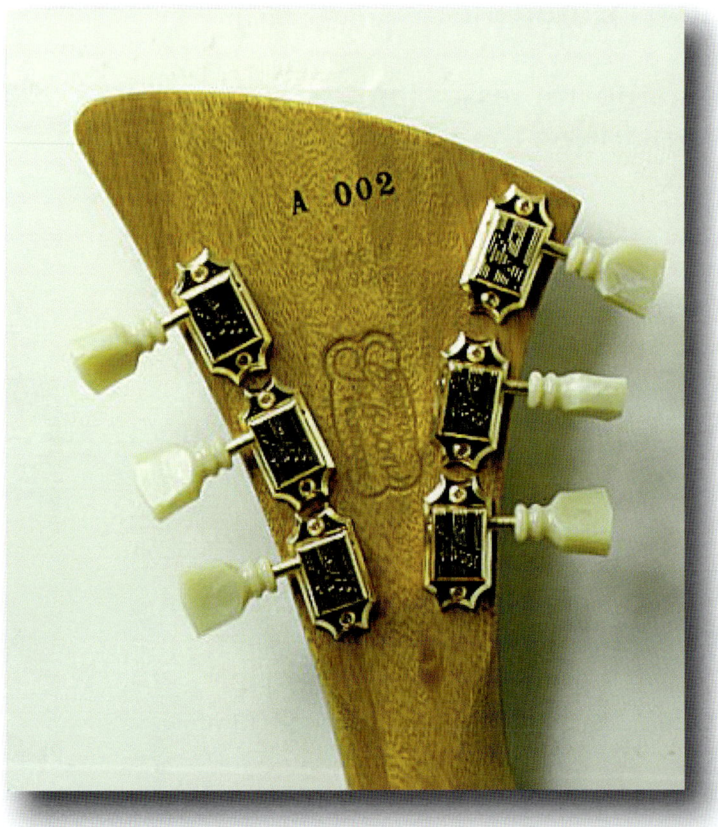

Photo credit:Ronny Burgett

Colors available were : Red, Natural Korina, Black, White

Photo credit:Elderly Instruments

A 1980 Prototype of the legendary Moderne and a 1954 EBO Violin Bass played by Olsie Robinson on Little Richard's early recordings.

Pictured on the left is Prototype number 82282021. It was owned by John Entwistle.
This instrument was produced on August 16th, 1982 in Kalamazoo, and was instrument #021 stamped that day

The guitar pictured is one of the first 6 made. At the 1982 NAMM show Gibson introduced the Heritage Series reissue of the Explorer, Flying V, and Moderne. This is one of six Moderne prototypes that were made for the show; the five others consisted of 2 Ebony, 1 Natural, 1 Sunburst, and 1 more Red. They were sequentially numbered 82282012-82282017.

Pictured is 82262015. .After the show, 500 of each of the Explorer, V, and Moderne were to be made, however it is believed that some Modernes were sacrificed for Flying V's because the V was more popular. As far as the guitar's origin, the story was that after the NAMM show it was given to Howard Leese who had been with the band Heart and endorsed Gibson, who later sold it through a music store in New Jersey in the 1980s.

Chapter 5
Fact Or Fiction?

GIBSON MODERNE: FACT OR FICTION?

Reprinted with permission from Vintage Guitar Magazine
September 1993 Page 38
By Cohn Rude

For years I've been on a quest to discover the truth behind the Moderne. Does one really exist in the basement of an unknown person, or is talk of their existence only a myth. I want to believe that they actually exist, but evidence for this is scant. The only alleged Moderne that has ever surfaced was one with the correct body, but an incorrect head stock. It was considered by everyone to be a fake and when it was copied by Ibanez and released on the open market in 1975. The waters were further muddied. If all the prototypes of the Gibson's modernistic guitars of this period were done in mahogany, including the Flying V, this accounts for the three most recent Futura's that have surfaced in mahogany.

Gibson's own shipping records show that 19 Modernes were shipped in 1958 and 3 were shipped in 1959. This doesn't account for all the 1957 and earlier prototypes and the working models that had already been developed. In studying photographs of Gibson templates one day I stumbled on to a real find. In one photo I discovered the templates for the bodies of the Futura and Moderne. It took some doing, but by enlarging and reducing the picture I was able to conclusively determine that the Moderne template had been laid upside down in the photo, on top of the Futura template and under the Flying V. So here I had my first piece of evidence for the existence of the Moderne. However, this is still not enough proof to prove the existence of the Moderne conclusively.

When Gibson reissued the Moderne which was prompted by Ibanez's release of the Destroyer (Explorer copy), Rocket Roll Sr.(flying V copy) and Model #2469 (The Moderne). Gibson itself got it wrong. The input jack was in the wrong location. They also erred with the pickguard, producing a smaller black one instead of a larger white pick guard which went up to the top of the pickup and back underneath the bridge, similar to the design used on the Flying V. The toggle switch was placed in the same place as the original. The gumby headstock was probably the death of the Moderne. It was just too weird looking. Had they given it the Flying V headstock or the Futura head stock it may have made it into production along with the Flying V and the Explorer. Gibson was granted a 4 year patent on these designs.

To begin my quest I set out acquiring every catalog Gibson published from 1957 to 1960, including Gazettes magazine ads. I found nothing to document the existence of this guitar. The Flying V appeared in the 1957 Gazette and the catalogue from 1958 and 1959. The Explorer appeared in the 1958 Gazette only. I ran into a dead end and my search seemed hopeless, but then some amazing things started to surface. I discovered that Gibson never filed for a patent without first having a prototype to work from. I concluded therefore that there must have been a working prototype of the Moderne.

Side by side comparison of the supposed real Gibson Moderne and the Ibanez Futura.

If we accept all of the above as plausible, the remaining question to be answered for the collector is how do we determine that the Gibson guitar he/she owns or is looking to purchase as a collector is, in fact, made by Gibson. If we insist on a strict rule that only those guitars produced by Gibson in the factory during factory working hours qualify, then very few, if any, Modernes or Futuras will fit this criteria. Gibson supposedly allowed employees to work on their own projects after hours. So, on the other hand, since many of the Modernistic guitars were put together by Gibson employees working after hours, we can only presume that these should be considered authentic Gibsons. It should also be pointed out that it was a common practice as Gibson's factory for guitars that had been developed in the Research and Development department be periodically purged (sold off, finished or unfinished). When Gibson moved the plant to Nashville, 12 bodies were sold, all Korina wood and modernistic design Flying V, Explorers, Futura and Moderne. Of course, any of these bodies which left the Gibson factory unassembled and later put together by an enterprising individual cannot be originals. I know of one Korina wood Moderne body and neck in a banjo makers shop on the east coast. Several years ago, an alleged Moderne was offered for sale at an asking price of $250,000. A bargain if you consider that a Japanese collector had offered one million dollars for an authentic Moderne. However, the instrument was never seen, thus no sale took place. In my opinion. Futuras are worth over $200,000, depending on the condition. Modernes, on the other hand, are priceless and are considered the rarest guitar in the world. Some compare it in value to the Stradivarius violin. If you are thinking about mortgaging your house to buy a Moderne, remember that it took ten years of research to come up with enough evidence where we can now be fairly certain that they exist. The Futura and Moderne never had hang tags which are used to document an instrument. Modernes also never had cases, another popular way to prove the authenticity of a guitar. And finally, so few Futuras have surfaced that it is difficult to compare muting channels. My advice is to leave the search for these two guitars to trained collectors who know what to look for.

New information has surfaced reveling that the Moderne could well have had 3 different head stock designs:The Gumby, The Futura Reverse V, and the Flying V Arrowhead stock. The Moderne in American Guitars is actually one of 3 made in 1963, the builders name will not be revealed to protect him. Two of the copy Modernes had Les Paul head stocks, one has a Gumby headstock and a serial number of 9-2416. All three are done in mahogany. The builder of these guitars learned the trade from an ex-Gibson employee, again name will have to be withheld to protect him. Although this gentleman was with Gibson during the development of the Futuristic Guitars, we don't know if he wound up with the original template for the Moderne. Sherman Music in Chicago remembers selling 3 Modernes of which one had a Futura Reverse V head stock, the other two had Gumby headstocks, with all three possessing large black pickguards, two with gold parts, one with nickel parts. Information was shared with me by the owner of an original Futura. He was shown a picture of a Moderne 10 years ago, but the person with the picture was unable to produce the guitar. I now believe the black pickguard Modernes were the original 1958's. The white pickguard Modernes were released in 1962.

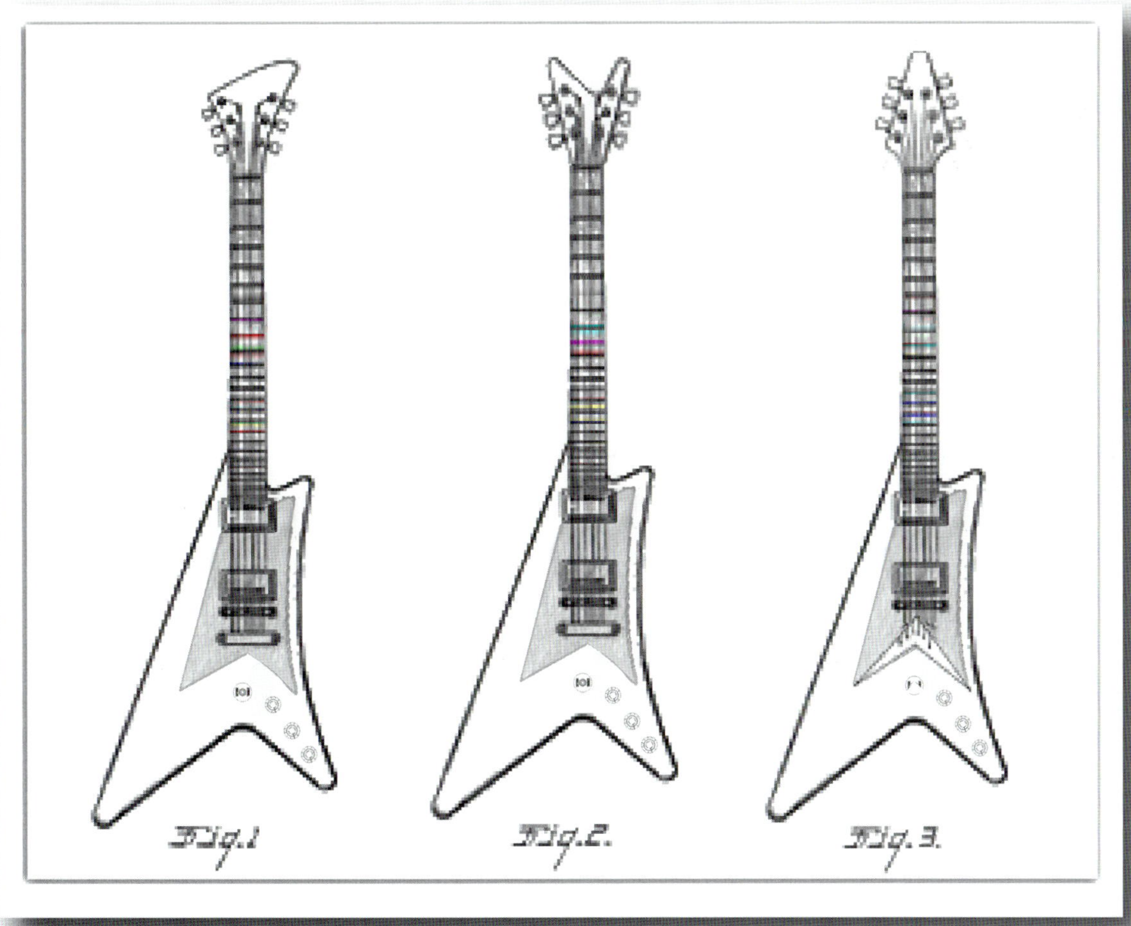

Chapter 6
The Reissue

The reissue of the Moderne was introduced only as a limited edition in the beginning of the 80's. Tim Shaw who worked on this project said the reissue model was built only based upon the patent application because nobody had any idea of the original. There was no one on the staff of Gibson from those days who remembered how many of them were built or how this guitar was made. They made the headstock a little bit smaller than the patent application diagram because it was too big for the production line. They also had to come up with the electric circuit and control parts based upon the Flying V or the Explorer parts that also had to be used on the Moderne.

All the reissue Gibson Modernes were made at the Gibson Kalamazoo plant in Michigan. At the time, the Kalamazoo plant was a soft tool plant where they could change tooling quickly to accommadate design changes. It was a better set up for producing prototype guitars than the Nashville hard tool plant which was set up for long production runs and tool changes were considerably more difficult to make. Prototypes were built as early as 1980.

Artist's sketch of the new Gibson plant addition. When completed, the factory will be one of the industrial showplaces in the Kalamazoo area.

Photo©Gibson

All of the first six prototype serial numbers are consecutive and are stamped in or impressed into the wood itself and carry the "original Gibson Prototype stamp" the prototype stamp.

According to the serial numbers, the first six prototypes were made in 1982 (except for the tobacco sunburst one that was reportedly seen at the 1982 NAMM show).

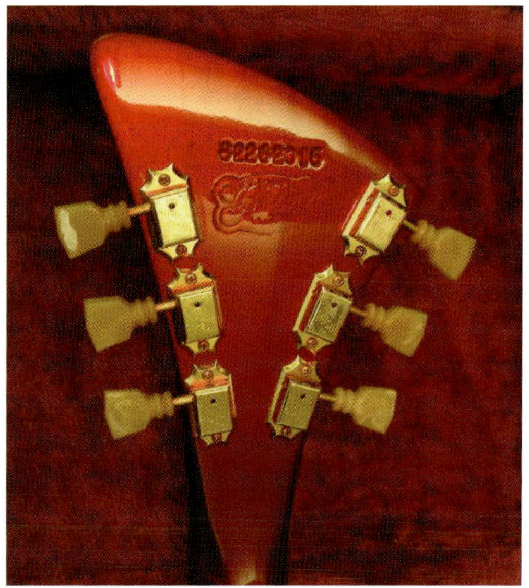

Stamped in 1982 serial number.
Notice the lack of the "Made in USA"

Inked on "A" series
serial number with "Made in USA"

Although the serial numbers 82262012- 82262016 were the earliest prototypes made, there are others that were made in Korina and have the A through H series inked on serial numbers where the serial numbers starts with a letter followed by a 3 digit number. They also bear the same Prototype stamp.

As early as 1980, Gibson decided to make the Moderne part of the Heritage series and built 6 prototypes: 1 natural Mahogany, 2 in black, and 2 in red. There is reason to believe that Gibson did not have a prototype Moderne at the NAMM trade show in 1981 as eyewitnesses at the 1981 NAMM show didn't recall seeing one. Several people say they saw a tobacco sunburst Moderne at the 1982 NAMM trade show, so it might exist but has not been verified.

The serial numbers for the first prototypes are:

- 82262012 color Red
- 82262013 color Black
- 82262014 color Black
- 82262015 color Red
- 82262016 color Natural Mahogany
- 82262017 color unknown
- 82282021 color Black
- 82282023 color Black

Gibson Kalamazoo didn't have the proper quantity of Korina in time for production in 1981. The Moderne serial number 82262016 is known to be made of Mahogany which may indicate some or all the prototypes were some other wood than Korina. The prototypes were built on August 14th, 1982 in Kalamazoo.

The Gibson Kalamazoo Factory

Unfinished guitars left over from the Kalamazoo Factory. These may have been intended to be finished in solid colors due to the fact that two appear to be made out of mahogany. Note the Futura style split head-stock on the far left. (see page 171)

A second batch of six prototypes with the serial numbers 82282018 to 82282023 came next followed by a third prototype run of modernes with the inked on serial numbers that were made of Korina. There were around 21 Korina Moderne prototypes made and had consecutive inked on serial numbers ranging from A 001-A 022 and also had an "Original Gibson Prototype " stamp, stamped into the wood in the center of the headstock. After the prototypes were ran, the serial numbers were set back to A 001 and then production started. The only factory colors on the Korina Moderne production run models with inked on serial numbers were Natual Korina, Ebony (black), and White. No one knows for sure exactly how many Modernes, prototypes or otherwise, were made.

G 454 *GIBSON, cont.*

MSR/NOTES	100% NEW	98% MINT	95% EXC+	90% EXC	80% VG+	70% VG	60% G	GRADING

MODERNE HERITAGE - single cutaway sharkfin style korina body, black pickguard, korina neck, 22-fret rosewood fingerboard with pearl dot inlay, tune-o-matic bridge/stop tailpiece, tulip blackface peghead with pearl logo inlay, inked serial number on peghead, 3-per-side tuners with plastic single ring buttons, gold hardware, 2 humbucker pickups, 2 volume/1 tone controls, 3-position switch, available in Natural, Red, White, or Ebony finishes, mfg. 1982-83.

	100%	98%	95%	90%	80%	70%	60%
	N/A	**$3,750**	**$3,350**	**$2,950**	**$2,600**	**$2,300**	**$1,950**

Initially, there were 500 guitars to be produced, but only 143 were actually manufactured. This is a reissue of the 1958 Moderne, with specifications from the blueprint.

ELECTRIC: MODERNE SERIES

MODERNE - originally designed as one of three Gibson modernistic concept guitars (with the Explorer and Flying V), this instrument was blue-printed in 1958. A debate still rages over whether or not they were actually built, as a 1958 Moderne has not yet been seen. There is some vague mention on a shipping list (that could also apply to the Explorer model). Tom Wheeler, in his book *American Guitars*, suggests that some were built - and when the music retailers responded in a negative way, Gibson sold some at a cut rate price to employees and destroyed others. Ted McCarty, who was president of Gibson at the time (and part designer of the three models), has guessed that a handful were built as prototypes.

It's hard to hang a price tag on something that hasn't been seen. Until one actually shows up, and is authenticated, values cannot be determined.

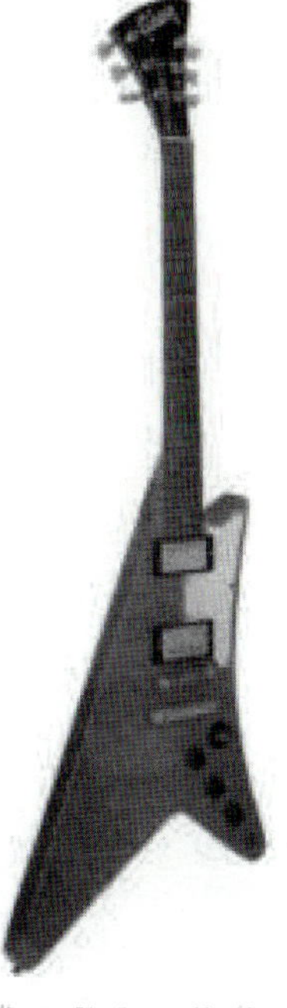

Gibson Moderne Heritage
courtesy Dave Rogers
Dave's Guitar Shop

According to the Blue Book of Electric Guitars by Zachary Fjestad, the total production estimate for the Heritage Moderne is around 143. Gibson had slated 500 Modernes to be made but stopped production due to of a lack of sales.

This is a Moderne prototype with the serial number 82282023. The original finish appears to have been Ebony.

This instrument was produced on August 16th, 1982 in Kalamazoo, and was instrument #023 stamped that day.

This is a body and neck that was never completed from the Kalamazoo Michigan Gibson Factory. The case is also from there. Gibson closed the Kalamazoo location in 1984 (last day in June).

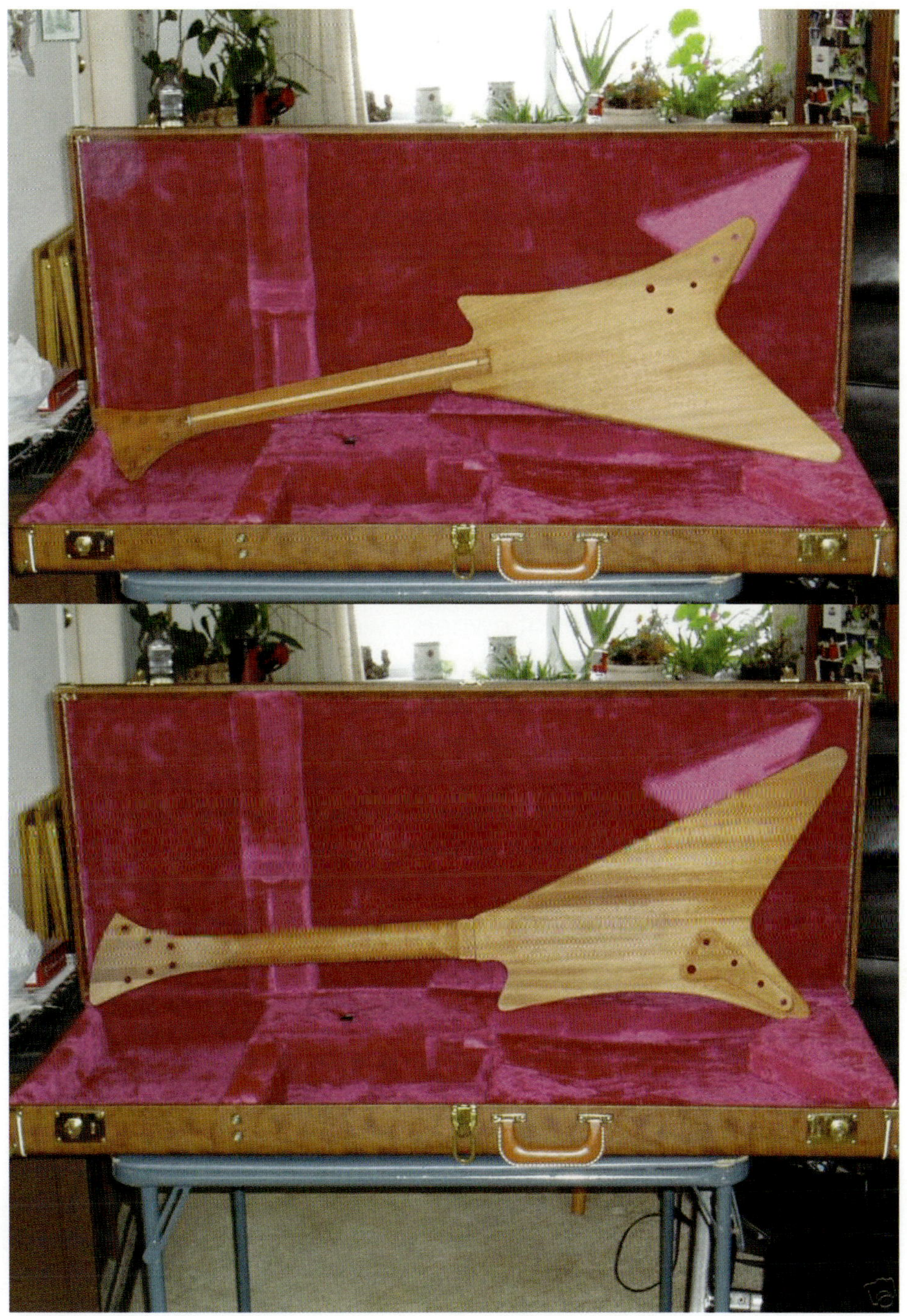

Towards the end of the closing of the Kalamazoo plant, items such as this were sold off.

In this close up of the pickups, we see that they are Patent Number 2737842. From interviews of owners, I was told that Gibson was using 300k ohm pots for the volume.

In the neck pickup cavity we see a stamp "Ant. Nat." This means the guitar was to be finished in an antique natural finish.

Mahogany prototype
serial number 82262016

Gibson considered doing the Heritage Korina reissue series in 1980. With the NAMM show coming up in 1981, Gibson wanted to debut the new Korina collection but they had one problem: there was no acceptable Korina wood in their stock and Gibson's buyers were having a difficult time finding quality Korina in the quantity they needed. In order to make the show, Gibson made some prototype Flying V's out of mahogany for the 1981 show.

1981 Mahogany Flying V prototype

Photos © Chris Grimmett of www.chrisguitars.com

The guitar pictured could be one of the first made or another example of a "built outside the Gibson factory" guitar. This instrument with serial number 81332501 was produced on May 13th, 1982 in Nashville and was instrument #1 stamped that day. If it is a genuine Gibson, it predates by three months all the other prototypes I've accounted for.

I sent an inquiry to Gibson regarding this particular guitar and their reply was: "The guitar does not have the peghead I would expect on a Moderne and the absence of "Made In USA" makes it suspect. It does not fit the description of any regular production model from 1982. It may have been a build out using a left-over body from the 1982-1983 Moderne. There is no record of any Moderne having a regular Gibson peghead."

This particular instrument has a lot of anomalies: chrome hardware, a bound fingerboard, no pickup selector ring, different tuners,different neck heel shape, different pickup cavities, different knobs,different control cavity. Comparison photos on the right are from a Heritage Moderne serial number A 057.

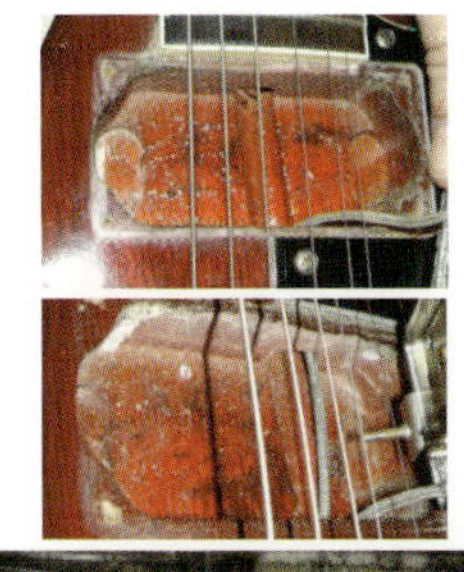

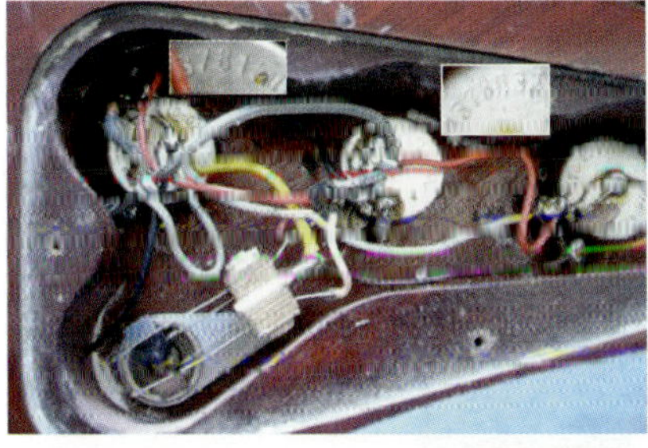

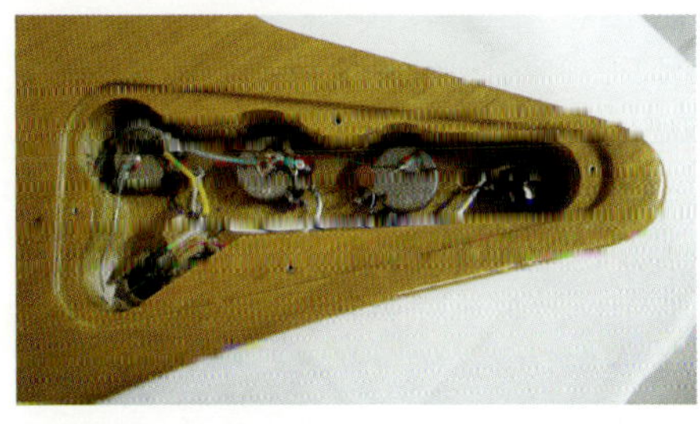

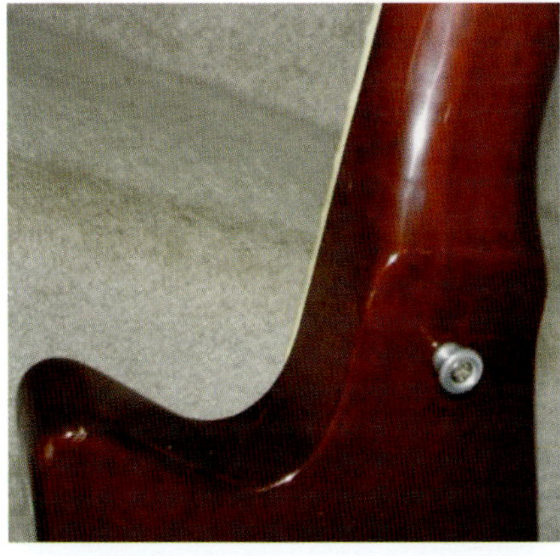

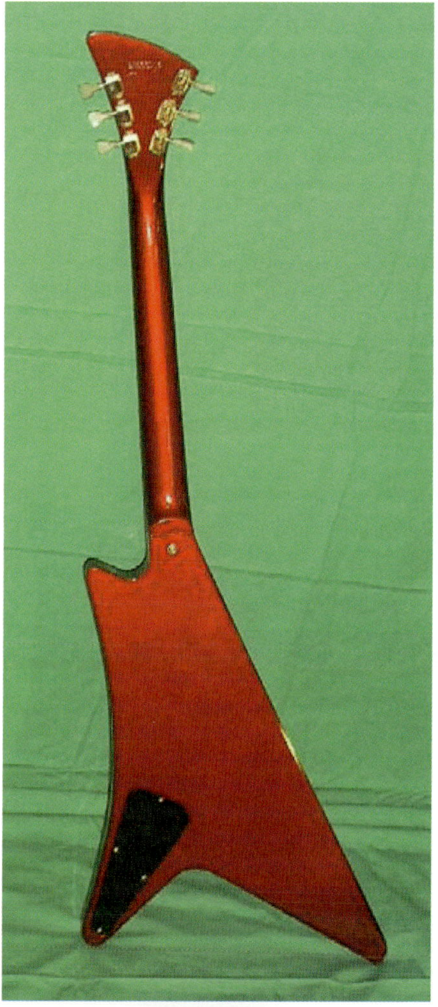

Moderne Prototype serial number 82262015

A view of the inside cavities of the Moderne

The reissue Moderne guitar has a very mysterious history. There was no one on the staff at Gibson from those days who remembers how many of them were built or how the guitar was made. The reissue of the Moderne was introduced only as a limited edition. Tim Shaw who worked on this project said the reissue model was built only based upon the patent application because nobody had any idea of the original. Tim Shaw remembers: "We made the head a little bit smaller than the patent application diagram because it was too big for the production line. And also we had to come up with the electric circuit and control parts based upon the Flying V or the Explorer."

Heritage Series advertisements

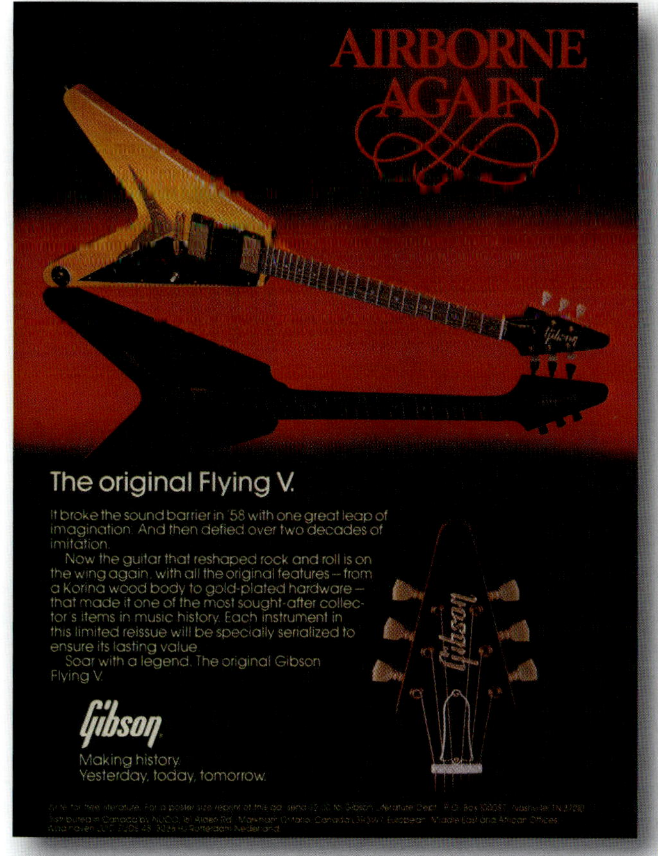

FOR YOUR RECORDS

Congratulations on owning your new Gibson musical instrument. For your own records, in case you ever need to identify your instrument for warranty or insurance purposes, fill out the following:

Model no.________________ Serial no. ________________

Date of purchase________ Dealer's name & address ________________

FOR OUR RECORDS

Your Gibson Warranty becomes effective when we receive the registration card filled out and signed by you. THE RETURN OF YOUR WARRANTY REGISTRATION CARD WITHIN 15 DAYS OF THE DATE OF ORIGINAL RETAIL PURCHASE IS A CONDITION PRECEDENT TO WARRANTY COVERAGE. We would also appreciate your taking a few extra moments to supply us with the additional information requested so that we can better serve you in the future.

GIBSON WARRANTY

Please supply requested information, sign and mail within 15 days of date of purchase. **Dealer Name**________________

1. Model number *Moderne ant nat*
2. Serial number *A-001* Lot No. *3022*
3. Last name____________ First____________
4. Address________________
5. City____________ State______ Zip______
6. Date of instrument purchase____________
7. Price paid:____________
8. What interested you in purchasing this instrument brand?
A ☐ teacher B ☐ friend C ☐ dealer D ☐ re-sale value E ☐ professional F ☐ tone quality G ☐ band or orchestral director H ☐ price J ☐ ease of playing K ☐ brand reputation L ☐ appearance M ☐ rental
9. What is your age______ and sex ☐ M or ☐ F
10. What type of music do you play?
A ☐ Rock B ☐ Country Western C ☐ Bluegrass D ☐ Jazz E ☐ Soul
F ☐ Band G ☐ Gospel H ☐ Folk J ☐ Classical K ☐ Orchestral
11. How many other instruments to you own?________
12. Did you make an instrument trade A ☐ yes B ☐ no
13. How often do you play:
1) Professional A ☐ less than twice a week B ☐ 2 times a week C ☐ full time
2) Personal pleasure A ☐ less than twice a week B ☐ 2 times a week C ☐ full time
3) If professional, how much income earned from performing
A ☐ 10% or less B ☐ 11-50% C ☐ 51-100%
14. How long have you been playing this type of instrument? ____ Years
15. How did you learn to play this instrument?
A ☐ school B ☐ private lessons C ☐ self taught D ☐ friend
16. How often do you attend live performances?

	Very Frequently	Frequently	Occa-sionally	Seldom	Neve
A Rock Concerts	1-☐	2-☐	3-☐	4-☐	5-☐
B Night Clubs	1-☐	2-☐	3-☐	4-☐	5-☐
C Band Concerts	1-☐	2-☐	3-☐	4-☐	5-☐
D Neighborhood Bars	1-☐	2-☐	3-☐	4-☐	5-☐
E Symphonies	1-☐	2-☐	3-☐	4-☐	5-☐
F Operas/Operettas	1-☐	2-☐	3-☐	4-☐	5-☐
G Recitals	1-☐	2-☐	3-☐	4-☐	5-☐

17. Are you currently taking lessons? A ☐ yes B ☐ no
If yes, where are you learning? C ☐ studio D ☐ private teacher E ☐ dealer F ☐ school
18. How did you first learn of this instrument?
A ☐ newspaper ad B ☐ magazine ad C ☐ radio/TV D ☐ band or orchestra director E ☐ played by professional F ☐ dealer G ☐ friend H ☐ teacher
19. What will be your next guitar purchase?

Owner's signature________________

The warranty and registration card for the very first production Moderne serial number A-001.

Gibson
A Division of Norlin Industries, Inc.
P.O. Box 100087
Nashville, Tennessee 37210
(615) 366-2400

March 19, 1985

Gibson®

Mr. Steve Hammond
1746 South Ferdinand Street
Seattle, Washington 98108

Dear Steve:

We appreciate your interest and your inquiry regarding the Gibson Moderne, serial # A-001.

Enclosed you will find a printed piece we researched and produced when we offered a limited series reissue of the Moderne. I hope you will find it informative and helpful.

Thanks for writing to us, and if we can be of further help, please let me know.

Best regards,

Randy Cullers
Manager
Artist Relations/Advertising

RC:ebm

Attach.

The prototype Moderne serial number A-001 was shipped by accident to Broadway Music. Upon realizing they had shipped the first prototype Korina Moderne by accident, Gibson called the store to retrieve the instrument. Unfortunately for Gibson, the guitar had already been sold.

December 1982 Vol. 1 No. 8 $2.00

Guitar Trader's®
VINTAGE GUITAR
Bulletin

Guitar Trader's Vintage Guitar Bulletin featuring the Gibson Heritage Moderne in Korina on the cover.

NEW ELECTRIC GUITARS:

NOTE: Our new guitar prices are the lowest we know of. We will try to beat or match any legitimate offer on any new guitar in our stock. If you do manage to find a lower price on a new guitar please call us! Prices in parenthesis are current manufacturer's list prices in effect at time of printing. Prices are subject to change without notice by manufacturer.

GIBSON: We have a large selection of models and colors in stock for immediate shipment. Call to order!

*__'59 Flametop__, The Ultimate Reissue! Highly-figured curly maple tops, all specs as per the original, a limited edition available only from Guitar Trader! See p. 18 for details. $1,595
Left-Handed model available. $1,695

*__Les Paul Deluxe__, set up like a Standard, but with mini-humbuckers for a special sound. Available goldtop, black, tobacco sunburst and natural ($1,009) $600

*__Les Paul Pro-Deluxe__, black or tobacco sunburst finish, with two soap-bar P-90 pickups. Ebony fingerboard! ($1,109) $655

*__Les Paul Standard__, large humbuckers, cream binding, crown inlay ($1,109) $655

*__Les Paul Custom__, gold-plated hardware, ebony fingerboard, large humbuckers ($1,209) $715

*__Les Paul Custom, nickel-plated hardware__, black, cherry sunburst, silver sunburst ($1,159) $685

*__Les Paul Custom__, Left-Handed, in stock cherry sunburst $795

*__LP 30th Anniversary__, goldtop, as advertised in Guitar Player ($1,329) $785
Optional one-piece mahogany neck ($1,429) $845

*__Flying "V"__, in stock natural mahogany and candy apple red $650

*__The "V,"__ all-maple body with binding and curly maple face. Available antique sunburst and antique cherry-burst $675

*__Flying "V" Heritage__, original Korina bodies in natural finish, black pickguard, copy of the original '58 "V", NOW IN STOCK! $795

*__Moderne Reissue__, "from the original mold", according to Gibson! Expected in soon — place your order now! $855

*__Doubleneck 6/12__ in stock in walnut! $1,090

*__ES-335 "Dot Heritage,"__ a re-issue of the historic '59 "dot-board" including that wide neck! ($1,128) $699
Left-Handed Dot Heritage model $800

*__ES-347__, in stock natural finish and black. Top-of-the line model with gold hardware, TP-6 adjustable tailpiece and Series VII humbucking pickups ($1,528) $885

*__Flying "V" Bass__, black finish ($999) $595

*__Chet Atkins Classical__, Gibson's new electric solid-body classical guitar ($1,119) $675

Call to order!

KRAMER:

*__Duke Standard Bass__, one humbucking pickup, 30¾" scale, 24 frets ($479) $350

*__Duke Special Bass__, 2 JBX pickups, 3-way tone switch, 24 frets ($579) $410

*__Duke Special Guitar__, 2 humbucking pickups, 25" scale, 22 frets ($579) $410

*__Pacer Carrera Guitar__, with Van Halen tremolo ($1,119) $670

*__Pacer Standard Guitar__, one humbucker, three way tone switch, tremolo, maple neck similar to a Strat $475

*__Pacer Custom Guitar__, two humbuckers, 22 frets, in stock in red finish! Standard Strat-style tremolo. $510

p. 22

FENDER: Models listed are in stock. Call for color availability.

*__Telecaster__, natural finish, rosewood neck in stock $490

*__Vintage Telecaster__, re-issue of the 1952 model, blonde, maple neck, bakelite black pickguard $595

*__Stratocaster__, with tremolo, maple or rosewood board ($895) $540

*__Stratocaster__, non-tremolo, maple or rosewood board ($840) $505

*__The Strat__, Brassmaster hardware, white pickguard. Available candy apple red, lake placid blue, white ($1,095) $660

*__Gold Strat__, gold hardware, 4-bolt neck $600

*__Stratocaster, Left-Handed model__, in stock sunburst, maple neck, with tremolo $650

*__'62 Stratocaster__, Vintage Strat reissue, sunburst finish, white pickguard, rosewood fingerboard $650

*__'57 Stratocaster__, Vintage Strat reissue, maple neck, two-tone sunburst. $650
Add $50 for Custom Finishes

*__Precision bass__, maple or rosewood fingerboard ($795) $480

*__Precision bass, Left-Handed__, in stock sunburst $595

*__Jazz bass__, maple or rosewood fingerboard ($920) $555

*__Jazz bass, Left-Handed__ in stock sunburst finish $675

Gibson

Firebird V

1. New style solid body and construction.
2. Two new performance humbucking pickups with nickel plated anti-magnetic nickel silver cover plates.
3. Brazilian rosewood fingerboard—with bound edges and pearloid inlaid position markers.
4. Sunburst mahogany finish.
5. New style Deluxe Vibrola by Gibson—heavy nickel plated.
6. Exclusive Gibson Tune-O-Matic bridge nickel plated with metal saddles.
7. Fine quality top grain cowhide, padded neckstrap.
8. White pickguard with attractive white, black, white, beveled edge.
9. Three position toggle switch with separate tone and volume controls for each pickup.
10. Extra heavy duty fine quality machine heads with metal buttons.

VERY LIMITED RE-ISSUE!

GIBSON FIREBIRD V

Now in Stock!!

GUITAR TRADER® and GIBSON GUITARS have done it again. We found fifteen (the last!) original Firebird tailpiece and parts assemblies at the Gibson factory in Kalamazoo, Michigan, and have had Gibson produce fifteen Firebird V's to fully original specifications. At this time we have them available in sunburst and white finishes. The colors are right and these guitars are hard to distinguish from originals! Call for further details.

AVAILABLE NOW
FOR IMMEDIATE DELIVERY!

SEND $1,250.
Trade-ins welcome.

PRINTED IN U.S.A.

Reprinted from original 1964 Gibson Catalog. Used with permission.

A page from Guitar Trader's Bulletin dated October 1982. In the left column, it states: "Moderne Reissue 'from the original mold', according to Gibson".

Moderne
Holy Grail of Vintage Guitars

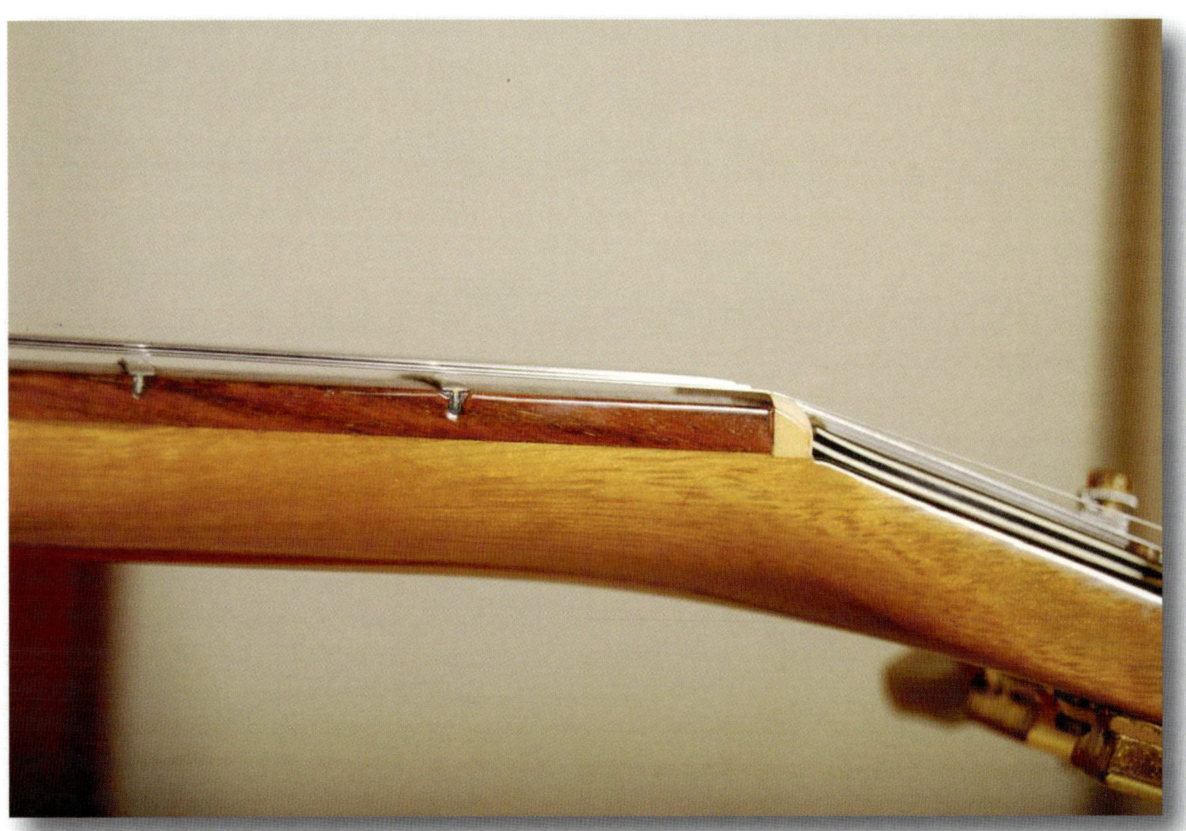

RHYTHM
TREBLE

Gibson

A 084

1671082

Chapter 7
The Copies

Epiphone®

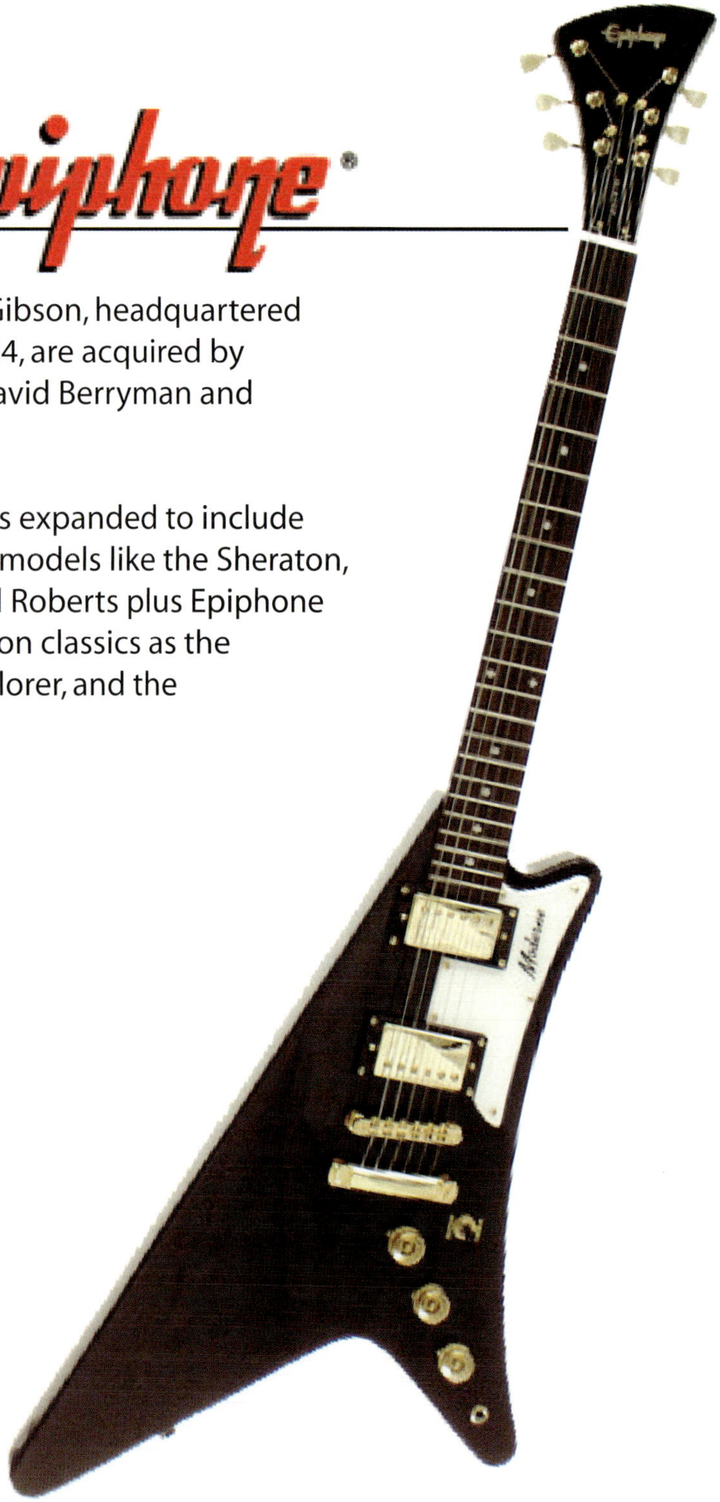

1986 Epiphone and Gibson, headquartered in Nashville since 1984, are acquired by Henry Juszkiewicz, David Berryman and Gary Zebrowski.

The Epiphone line has expanded to include traditional Epiphone models like the Sheraton, Emperor and Howard Roberts plus Epiphone versions of such Gibson classics as the Les Paul, Flying V, Explorer, and the Moderne.

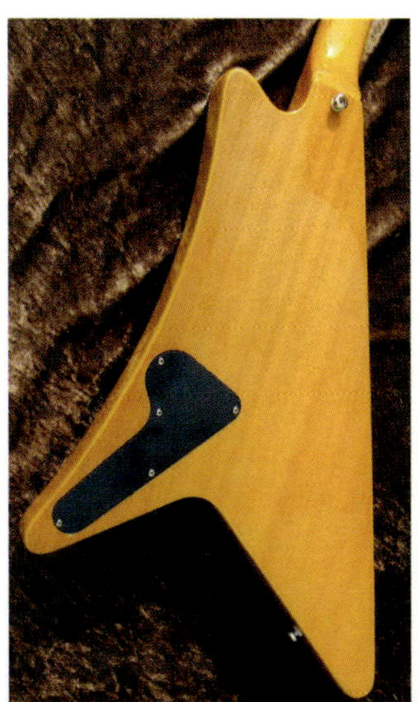

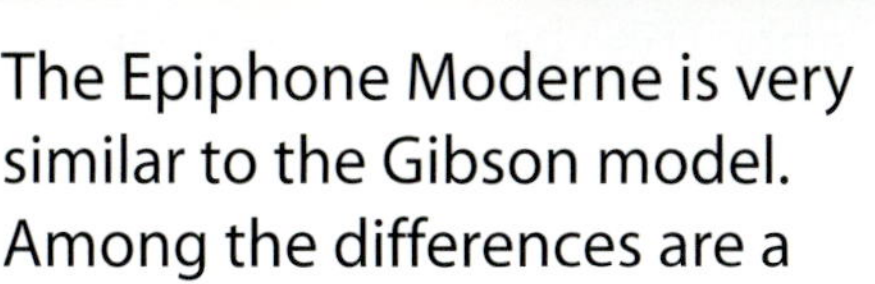

The Epiphone Moderne is very similar to the Gibson model. Among the differences are a printed pickguard, a different cavity cover, slightly altered headstock, truss rod cover, toggle switch tip, neck heel, and of course, the headstock logo.

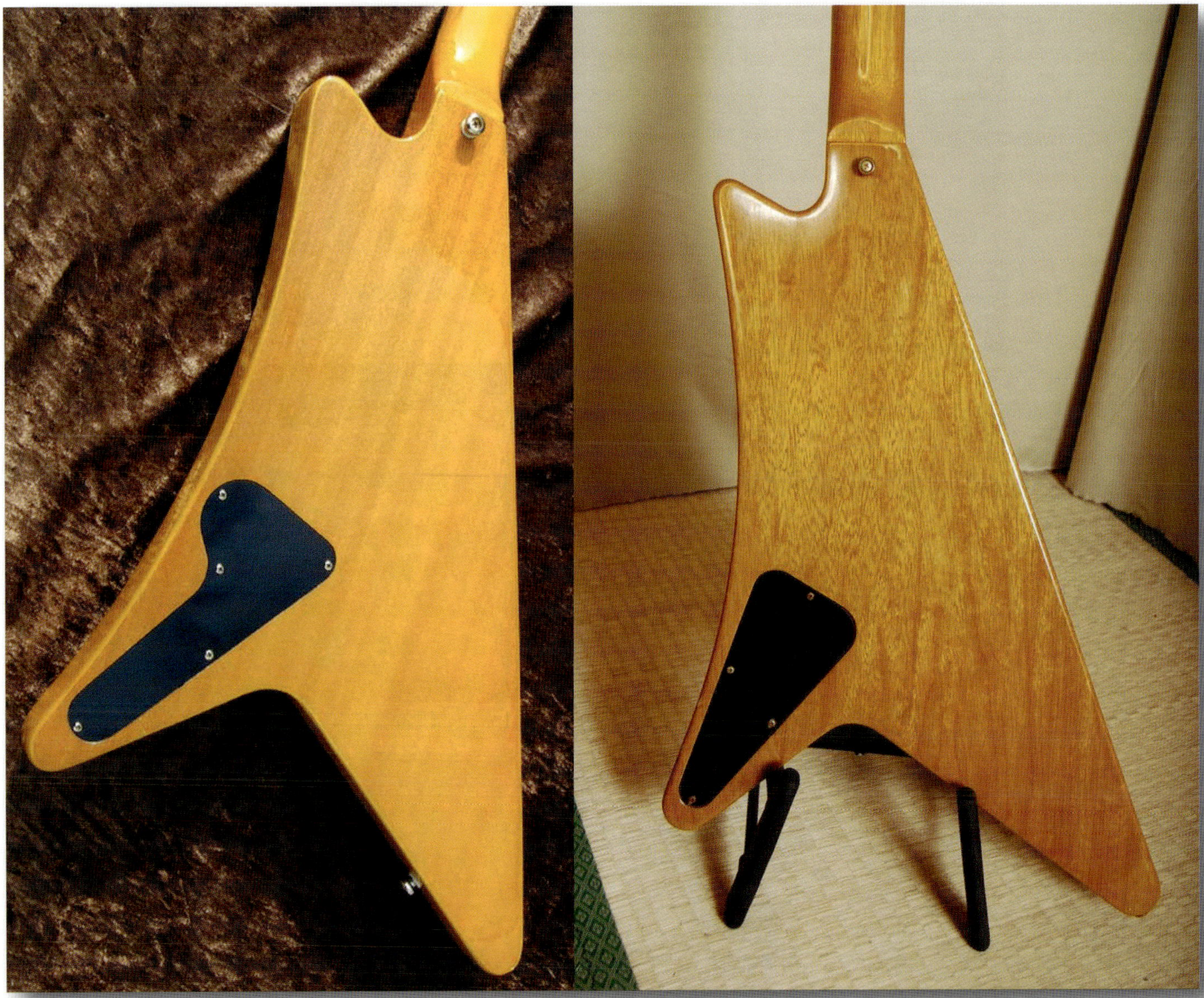

Subtle differences are noticed between the Epiphone guitar on the left and the Gibson Moderne on the right. The control cavity and cover on the Epiphone differs considerably. The shape of the neck heel is more rounded on the Gibson.

Moderne

Epiphone serial numbers give the following information:

An "I" at the beginning means manufactured by Sae In (Korea);
"U" means by Unsung (Korea); "P" means Peerless (Korea); "
"S" means Samick (Korea);
"R" is manufactured by "Peerless Guitars" of Korea.
DW = DeaWon (China); EA = Gibson/QingDao (China);
EE = Gibson/QingDao (China); MC = Muse (China); SJ = SaeJung (China);
BW = China
"B" (found on some Korina G-400 is Bohêmia Musico-Delicia (Czech Republic);
SI = Samick Indonesia
F = Fujigen (Japan)

Example: U8034853 U= Unsung 8= 1998 03 = March 4853= manufacturing number

Compare the fronts of the headstocks of the Epiphone and the Gibson. The Epiphone has a three screw truss rod cover, single ring style tuners. The top left of the Epiphone headstock is more rounded.

This is the Epiphone Moderne in a black finish.

The USA Collection: Limited Edition

Now in production is the limited edition USA Collection featuring four guitars designed by celebrated instrument designer Kurt Hendrick who has made guitars for rock's elite. He was commissioned by Epiphone to create an extreme line of guitars, the USA Collection.

Each of the four guitars -- Moderne, Comet, Apollo and Futura -- play off famous Gibson shapes, but with Kurt's skilled hand and imagination, these guitars are taken to the extreme.

The Moderne offers the classic body shape; the Comet is Kurt's own Modern-influenced design; the Apollo features an altered Flying V shape, and the Futura is a classic Gibson body shape which was invented in 1957, along with the original Flying V and Moderne (It became the Explorer years later).

One of the most profound features of the USA Collection is that the pickguards are recessed into the guitar's body. This affords a completely flat top and makes pickguard an integral part of the guitar.

The Collection also features nitrocellulose lacquer finishes, bound tops, Select grade Indian Rosewood fingerboards, and eye-splitting body designs. Assembled in USA, the USA Collection offers a high quality guitar at an excellent price.

Exclusive features include:

Moderne: Classic body shape, solid tone wood construction, a bolt-on neck, 25.50" scale. nitrocellulose lacquer finish, copper metallic painted top, Ivory color binding, Ivory color inlaid pickguard, Walnut stained back, antique natural hard maple neck, Floyd Rose locking tremolo, mini-Grover tuners, select grade, Indian rosewood fingerboard, EXP-S headstock, pearloid dot fingerboard inlay, two covered PAF humbucker pickups.

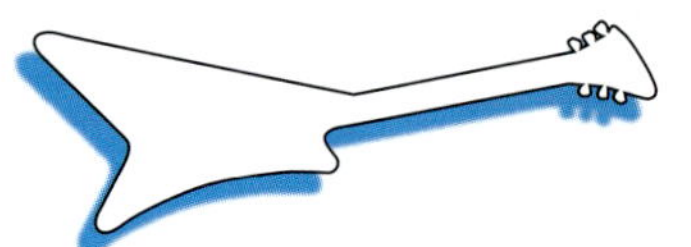

The other three models in the USA Collection.

APOLLO

COMET

FUTURA

Epiphone

The "Polyester Series"
Limited Edition

The Polyester Series guitars are like the finest racing cars...built for speed and offering plenty of eye candy. Under the hood, these guitars feature a long-scale, wider and flatter neck; a wide radius Indian Rosewood fingerboard, super low action, jumbo fret wire, satin finish, and a Floyd Rose tremolo and locking nut.

Their fast looks come from the unique polyester finish, a super clear-super hard finish that allows the grandeur of the guitar's flamed and figured top to shine through.

The "Polyester Series" includes the Poly Mod (a hot-rodded Moderne), the Poly V (a hot-rodded Flying V) and the Poly X (a hot-rodded Explorer).

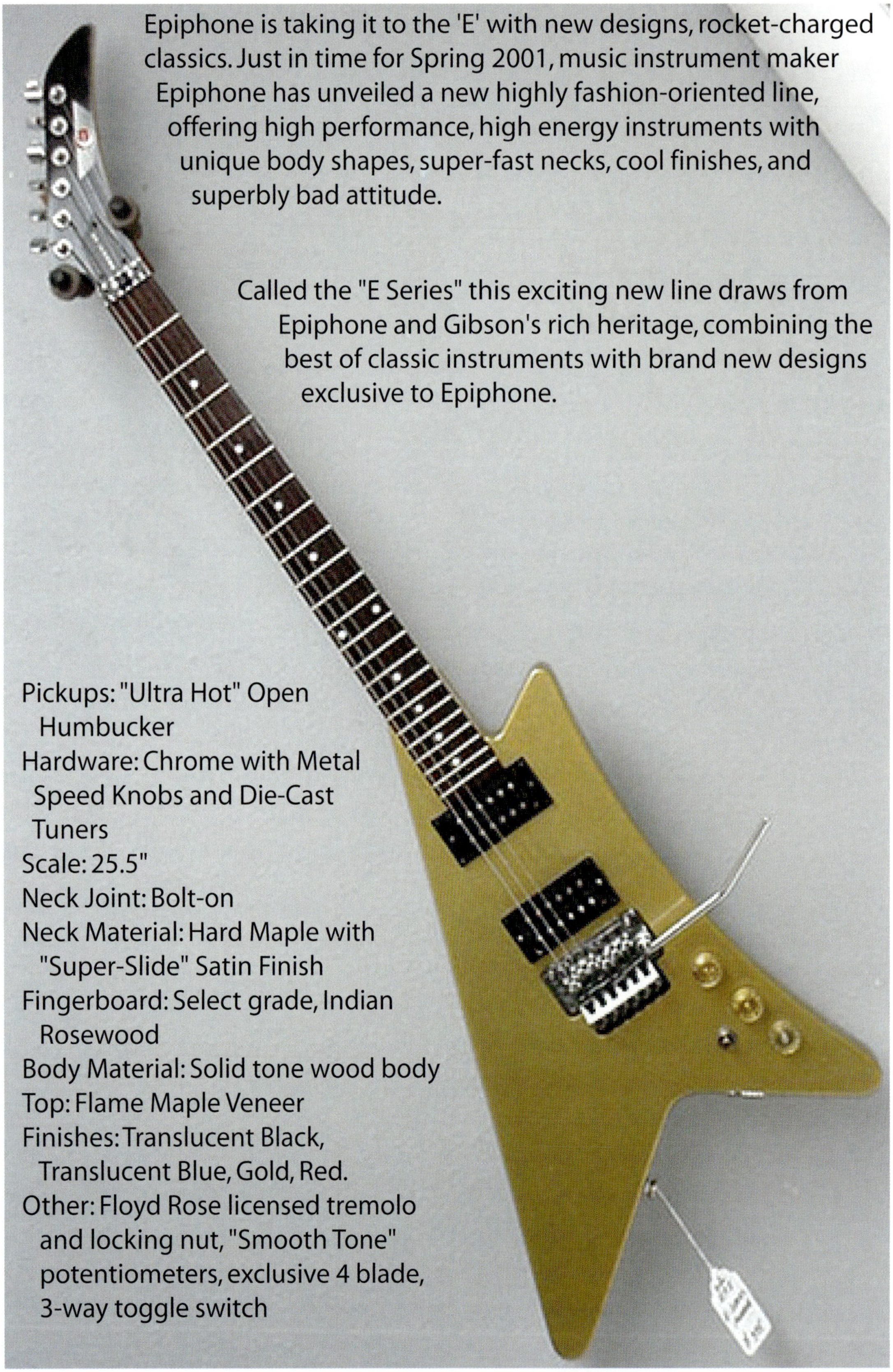

Epiphone is taking it to the 'E' with new designs, rocket-charged classics. Just in time for Spring 2001, music instrument maker Epiphone has unveiled a new highly fashion-oriented line, offering high performance, high energy instruments with unique body shapes, super-fast necks, cool finishes, and superbly bad attitude.

Called the "E Series" this exciting new line draws from Epiphone and Gibson's rich heritage, combining the best of classic instruments with brand new designs exclusive to Epiphone.

Pickups: "Ultra Hot" Open Humbucker
Hardware: Chrome with Metal Speed Knobs and Die-Cast Tuners
Scale: 25.5"
Neck Joint: Bolt-on
Neck Material: Hard Maple with "Super-Slide" Satin Finish
Fingerboard: Select grade, Indian Rosewood
Body Material: Solid tone wood body
Top: Flame Maple Veneer
Finishes: Translucent Black, Translucent Blue, Gold, Red.
Other: Floyd Rose licensed tremolo and locking nut, "Smooth Tone" potentiometers, exclusive 4 blade, 3-way toggle switch

This is the Epiphone
Mo Baby.

These came with a built in amplifier, full scale bolt on neck, and one humbucking pickup.

Mo'Baby

Epiphone
GIBSON

Epiphone

Ibanez

In 1932, the Hoshino Gakki Ten, Inc. factory produced musical instruments under the name Ibanez. The Ibanez trademark originated from the Fuji plant in Matsumoto, Japan. Ibanez produced guitars in Japan in the early 1960s, and some models were produced in Korea since 1980.
Ibanez guitars were distributed in the U.S. by Ibanez USA (Hoshino) in Bensalem, Pennsylvania. Other distribution offices include Quebec (for Canada), Sydney (for Australia), and Auckland (for New Zealand).
In the 1960's, Hoshino was producing instruments under various trademarks such as Ibanez, Star, King's Stone, Jamboree, and Goldentone.

In the mid 1950s, Harry Rosenbloom opened the Medley Music store outside Philadelphia. As the Folk Music boom began in 1959, Rosenbloom decided to begin producing acoustic guitars and formed the Elger company (named after Rosenbloom's children, Ellen and Gerson). Elger acoustics were produced in Ardmore, Pennsylvania between 1959 and 1965.

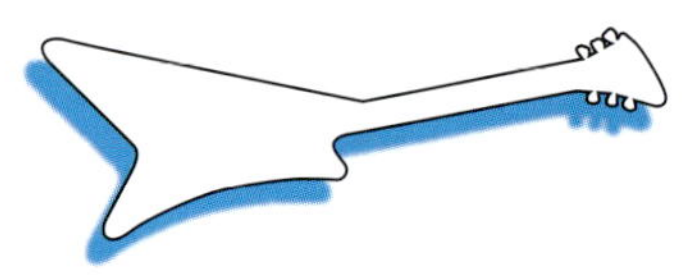

In the 1960s, Rosenbloom travelled to Japan and found a number of companies that he contracted to produce the Elger acoustics. Later, he was contacted by Hoshino to form a closer business relationship. The first entry level solid body guitars featuring original designs first surfaced in the mid 1960s, some bearing the Elger trademark, and some bearing the Ibanez logo. One of the major keys to the perceived early Ibanez quality is due to Hoshino shipping the guitars to the Elger factory in Ardmore. The arriving guitars would be rechecked, and set up prior to shipping to the retailer. Many distributors at the time would just simply ship "product" to the retailer, and let surprises occur at the unboxing. By reviewing the guitars in a separate facility, Hoshino/Ibanez could catch any problems before the retailer so the number of perceived flawed guitars was reduced at the retail/sales end. In England, Ibanez was imported by the Summerfield Brothers, and sometimes had either the "CSL" trademark or no trademark at all on the headstock. Other U.K. distributors used the Antoria brand name, and in Australia they featured a "Jason" logo.

In the early 1970s, the level of quality rose to equal those of the American designs. The Ibanez reproductions of Stratocasters and Les Pauls was at least equal and some say better than the quality of Norlin era Gibsons or CBS era Fenders. The unauthorized reproductions eventually led to Fender's objections to Tokai's imports leading to the infamous "headstock sawing" incident, and Norlin taking Hoshino into court for patent infringement. When Ibanez began having success reproducing Gibson guitars and selling them at a lower price on the market, Norlin, who was Gibson's owner at the time, sent a cease and desist warning. Norlin's lawyers decided that the best way to proceed was to defend the decorative (the headstock) versus the functional (body design), and on June 28th, 1977 the case of Gibson vs. Elger Co. opened in Philadelphia Federal District Court. In early 1978, a resolution was agreed upon: Ibanez would stop reproducing Gibsons if Norlin would stop suing Ibanez. The case was officially closed on February 2, 1978.

The infringement lawsuit ironically might have been the kick in the pants that propelled Ibanez and other Japanese builders to get back into original designs. Ibanez stopped building Gibson exact reproductions, and moved on to other designs. By the early 1980s, certain guitar styles began appealing to other areas of the guitar market and Ibanez's use of famous endorsers probably fueled the appeal. Ibanez's continuing program of original designs and artist involvement continued to work in the mid to late 1980s, and continues to support their position in the market today.

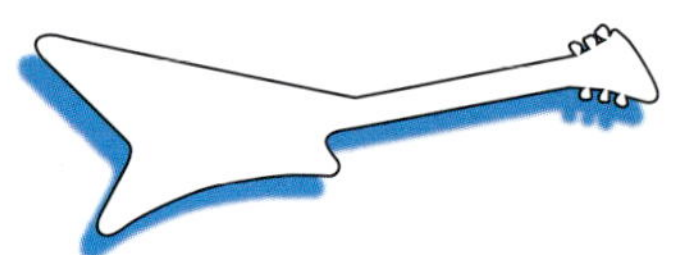

A mid 70's magazine ad featuring a trio of Ibanez

Notice the relief carved into the lower half of the body. The Black Moderne that Dan Erlewine owned had this same feature (see page 127).

Moderne
Holy Grail of Vintage Guitars

Ibanez

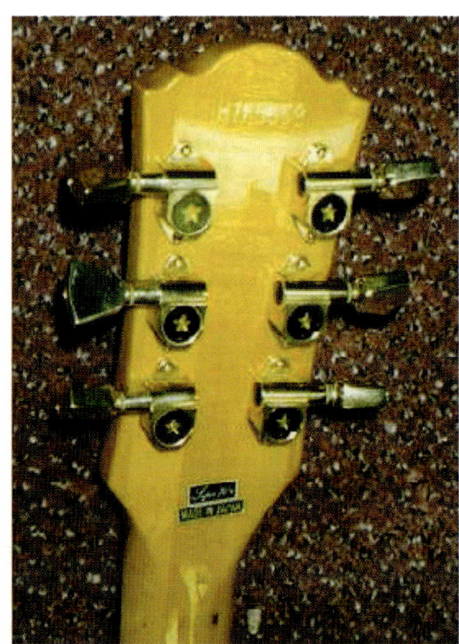

Ibanez

Here are two different Ibanez Futura's but with subtle differences. The one on the left has gold hardware and what appears to be black "top hat" knobs and the strap button at the very end of the body.

The Ibanez Futura on the right has chrome hardware and "witch hat" knobs and a darker, "aged" toggle switch tip and the strap button is moved closer inwards from the end of the body.

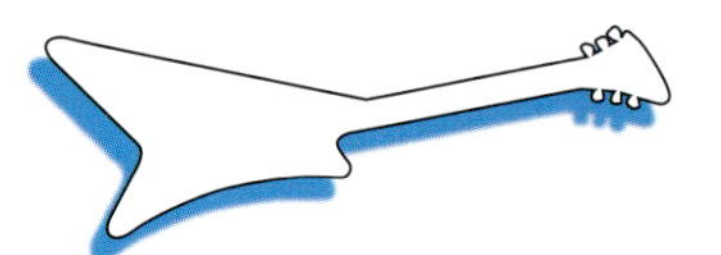

The back of this headstock of the Ibanez Futura shows the serial number clearly.

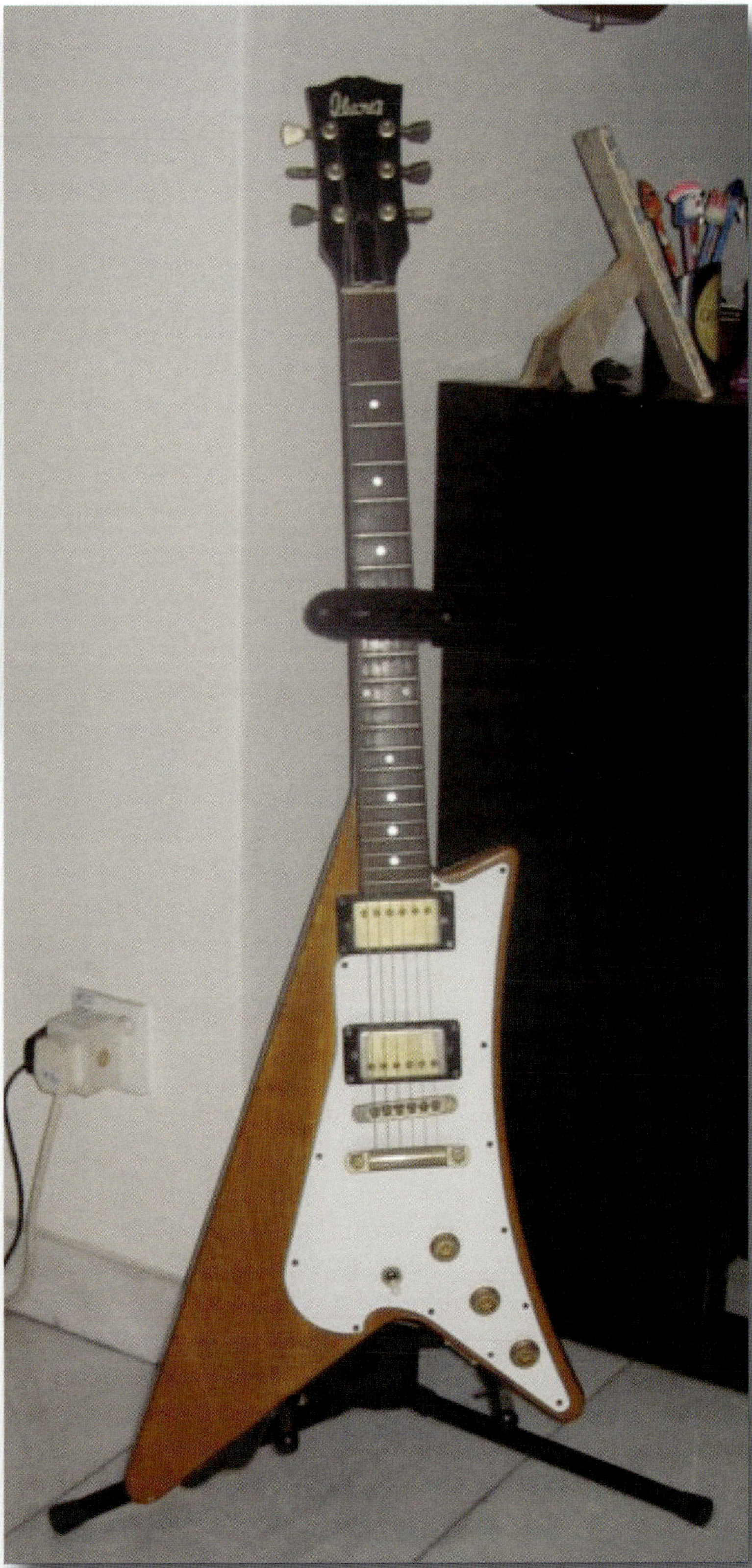

Photo ©Steve Kellett

Side by side comparison of two Ibanez Futuras.

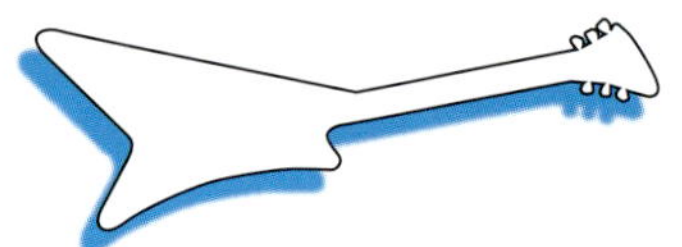

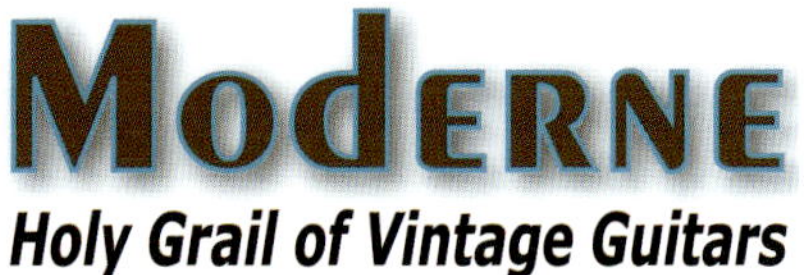

Greco was one of the earliest "lawsuit" guitar makers in Japan. They have been making guitars since the early 1960's at the FijugenGakki plant. Most of the 1960's guitars were original models, but in the early 1970's, they got into making replicas of original Fenders and Gibson's. At first, they didn't have the hardware to make really good, exact replicas, but by 1974 or so, they had the correct-style hardware to match their excellent craftsmanship, and they put out some killer replicas. Also, Greco made more clone models of original Fender, Gibson, Rickenbacker, Gretsch, Zemaitis, Ibanez, and other brands, than all other companies combined. They beat Tokai to the lawsuit race by at least five years.

Eventually, as the company found that the demand for their popular replicas grew and that the size of the production was getting too large, they relinquished their Stratocaster division to Fender Japan in late 1981. By 1982, Greco Stratocasters became Fender JV Stratocasters, then later MIJ and CIJ Stratocasters, made by the same guys who made the Greco "Sparkle Sound," "Spacey Sound," "Sparkle Sound," and "Super Real" Stratocasters from 1977-1981.

Greco still retained the business of selling great Gibson copies and other brand knockoffs of extraordinary high quality up until 1989. After that, the pressure to "cease and desist" production of copyright-infringing designs took its toll on Greco and they decided to change their headstocks and logos to avoid a confrontation with the American manufacturers. Greco would no longer make any exact reproductions of Gibson guitars.

They are becoming extremely rare and the demand is getting greater by the month for these older Greco guitars. The most collectible by far are the "Super Real" (made in 1980 only) and "Mint Collection" (made from 1981-1990)models, which were made to amazing likeness to original Fenders and Gibson's. Greco's 1977-1979 clones are very nice, too, but many have hardware and specs that don't match up with the Gibson and Fender classic designs.Many guitar magazines printed in Japan recently illustrate this demand. "Japan Vintage" is one of the new magazines printed and dedicated for the sole purpose of highlighting these beauties. Collectors around Japan lend their guitars for pictures and experts lend their stories to gather a very good history of the companies and interesting tidbits of knowledge.

Greco serial numbers:

The letter that (may) begin the serial number corresponds with the month of production, and the next 2 digits tell the year. For example: E804235 would be a May, 1980 "Super Real" model, production number 4,235.

Sometimes, Greco didn't use letters and only numbers, and even separated the first digit from the rest on occasion. When the first digit is separated, it is likely a 1980's model; the separated digit corresponding to the year of the 1980's in which it was made.

*If there is no serial number stamped into the wood (not on a sticker), it was made in Korea.

No serial number on this Greco Moderne.

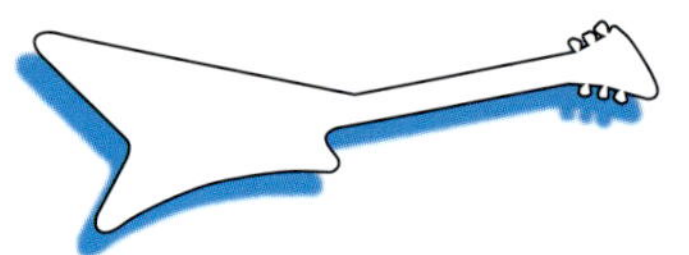

MD900 ············ ¥80,000
●ピックアップ／U-2000×2●ボディ／セン●ネック／メイプル●セットネック●指板／ローズウッド●3段階切替スイッチ●V×2, T×1●ナチュラル仕上

From the 1976 Greco catalog we not only see their copy of the Moderne, but also the Explorer, and the Flying V.

Notice the pickup covers are removed.

Moderne
Holy Grail of Vintage Guitars

Greco

ANTORIA

In the UK in the late 70's FCN and Summerfield were the importers of Antoria and Ibanez guitars respectively. To some degree, Antoria were just rebadged Ibanez models. E.g. the 3 P/U SG custom copy 2345WH was released with an Antoria logo on the headstock. Both guitars are exactly the same . Antoria models were made of slightly lower grade materials. Antoria copies seemed to appear more as Ibanez started to release their Artist and Professional models.

In 77/78 there was a definite transition period between the two brands as there must have been some left over Ibanez copies around (Les Paul copies spring to mind). The Ibanez pickups had Super 70 engraved on the bottom of the plates; the Antorias had a number stamped on the bottom (15723). Other than that they were identical.

H.S. Anderson

Made by Vestax in Japan circa 1978.

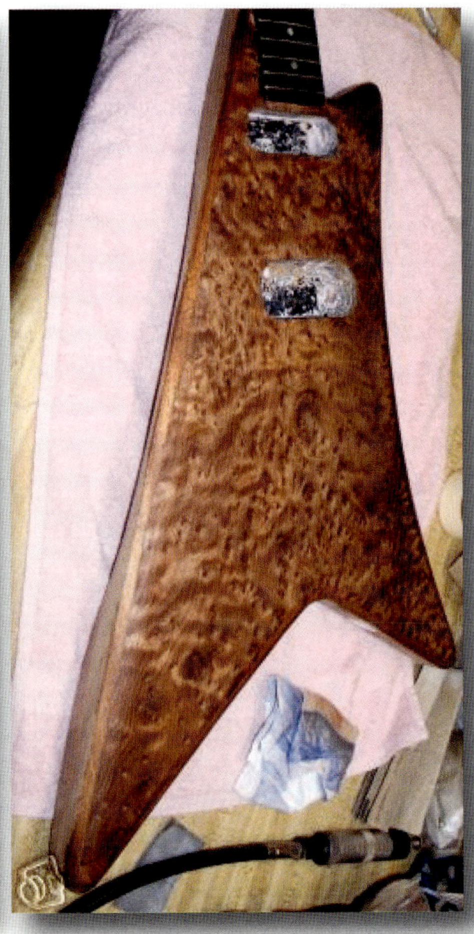

This is a new Moderne made by Haik.

DEFIL

The Defil Kosmos was a Polish copy of the Gibson Moderne with a different shape of headstock and a bolt-on neck. Manufactured at the Fabryka Lutniczych,The Lower Silesian Factory of Luthiery in Lubin, a city in western part of Poland. Defil started in 1896 as a piano production factory then and is presently not in as good economic shape as before. Kosmos guitars were manufactured during the 1980's. They were a favorite guitar of Polish heavy metal bands.

Body: alder; Neck: maple, bolt-on; Fretboard: rosewood, 21 frets
Pickguard and dot inlays: white plastic; Pickups: 2 humbuckers
Controls: volume, tone, tone, pickup selector;

Will Ray's eBay Strategies
© By Will Ray / Guitar Player January 2004

Auction Item: 1982 Gibson Moderne Winning Bid: $510.This is one of the strangest guitars I ever purchased on eBay. This particular one was listed as a "player's guitar," which is always a sign of trouble. The auction description said it had a Korina body that had been painted over with a refrigerator-white primer (another sign of trouble), and the bridge, tailpiece, and neck pickup were taken from some old, undisclosed 1969 Gibson guitar. More bad news: a broken headstock (that had been professionally repaired), a missing Gibson logo, various parts of the body "filled in with wood filler," and "bullet holes" in the upper neck that had been filled in with rosewood dowels. The bridge pickup was a '58 Gibson PAF reissue, with new Gibson pots, tuners, and a selector switch thrown in. That was the good news. After scoring the guitar for $510 (and $20 shipping), I decided to sand off the ugly white primer and repaint the Moderne in a faded, '50s-style Gretsch White Penguin hue.

Fig. 1

When the old primer was stripped off, I was shocked to see that the entire guitar had been sawed into three separate pieces, and later glued back together. After a little investigation, I learned that Gibson used to take their reject guitars and cut them up to discourage dumpster divers from reconstructing them.
Obviously this guitar had a will to live. To my surprise, my painter friend did an amazing job. He only charged $250, and he even put a Gibson decal on the headstock before clear coating it. What a guy! I also had my repair guru, John Wescott, do a much needed setup—which raised my total cost for the Moderne to $840.

So is it a keeper? Absolutely! The neck plays like a 20-year-old Gibson that has been broken in nicely, and the pickups sound awesome with lots of warmth and punch. This started out as a rescue mission, but now I have a guitar with a good story behind it.

Three prominent vintage guitar experts examined this guitar and declared this guitar to be a fake. Here is the story from Erick Coleman: "A few years back Dan received a call from a man who honestly believed that he had found a "prototype" Moderne on Ebay. He had spoken to the seller/owner on numerous occasions about the guitar and was convinced it was genuine.

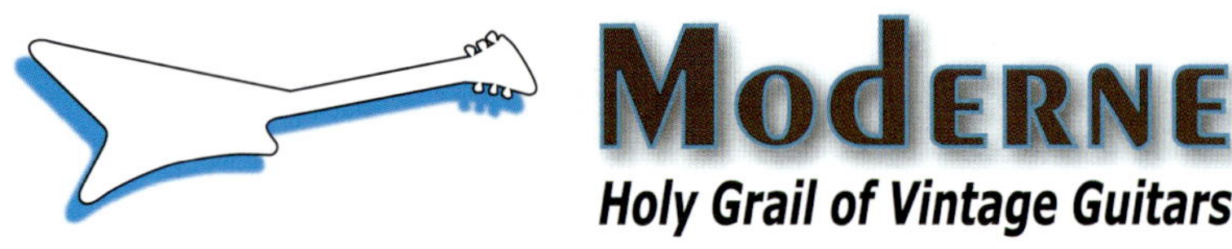

The seller (a guy named Mike) had given this fellow the impression that he was sitting on the lost "million dollar guitar" everybody had been looking for.

Now, this fellow didn't want to buy the guitar, he wanted to write a book about the 50's oddities. He had done a ridiculous amount of research on the Korina models, such in-depth stuff that he actually had a books worth of details, real dork level stuff.

In any case, he offered to help the seller move the guitar in exchange for cash and letting him write about it.

Now this guy (who Dan and I can't even remember his name), decided that he needed the guitar authenticated before he would look for a potential buyer, that's where Dan came in. he asked if he and the seller could bring the guitar down here for a hands on evaluation. Dan said he'd like to have Tom Murphy and Phil Jones on hand to assist so the guy made arrangements to get them to town as well.

So, on a rainy Saturday afternoon. Dan, Tom, Phil, Gene Imbody and myself (probably a few more) converged on Dan's to see this guitar.

After a long winded introduction, the guy finally opened the case. There were several obvious signs on the surface that didn't look like Gibson work, once the guitar was opened up there were other issues such as incorrect routs, metric parts, etc. After two hours of looking at the guitar Phil said "I'm real sorry, but this just doesn't look like work that Gibson would have done." Everyone else agreed.

We all got the impression that the seller knew it was fake all along. He was just seeing if a luthier buddy could fool the heavies. The guitar has been spotted on Ebay from time to time (along with a Futura knock-off), but listed as a "possible" Max instead of a prototype. What a load, it's not even close to a Max.

It did have a "Gumbyish" peghead which was our first visual tip off on it being a fake. The thickness, the way the truss rod cavity looked, the spruce veneer. I'm not sure why the guy didn't want us to take photos. I remember feeling like the fellow might not have believed us when he was initially told it was not real. It wasn't until several days later that we heard from him and he said he felt as if he had been given the run-around by the seller.

I'll try to find the guys name. I know Dan doesn't remember it but there is a poster around here somewhere that was a mock up of his book cover, and he had Dan, Phil and Tom sign it along with himself. I'll see if I can decipher his signature and hunt for his email address in my email folder. I was in contact with him a couple of times after his visit here.

The guy had done a huge amount of research, talking to old Gibson guys, documenting stories about the Moderne from guys who claimed to have seen them. I remember him commenting that he had alienated his family with his Moderne obsession and was in considerable hot water over the whole event. He spent a good amount of money out of his own pocket to bring in and accommodate Phil and Tom.

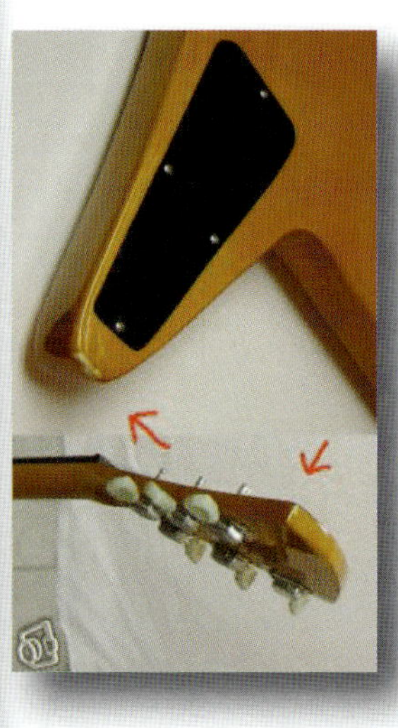

This Moderne appeared on Ebay in 2008

Chapter 8
The Proof?

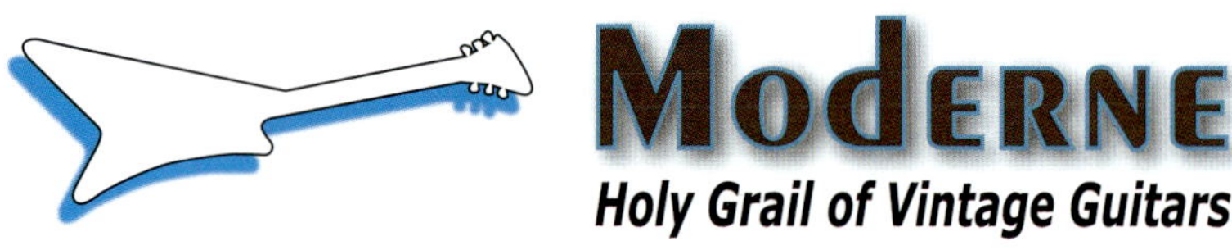

The world's shortest interview w/ Billy F. Gibbons

http://www.universalmetropolis.com/city/threads.php?threadid=14435

Background: as previously discussed I am a fan of Guitars in general, and specifically the Flying V. They Flying V is part of a series of 3 innovative instruments introduced by Ted McCarty during his redirection of Gibson Guitars in 1957. These were the futuristic line of instruments which includes the iconic Flying V, its even less common freaky sister, the Explorer, and the ultra-mysterious Moderne. While patent diagrams of all three exist and limited numbers of V's and Explorers were made between 1957 1959, the Moderne was never officially produced, and while no record exists of any leaving the factory, rumor abounds that surely 3 or 4 or 5 prototypes were likely constructed, and some exists today.

The mystery of this phantom 3rd design captivated me early on, and I looked into it. I found that Gibson had released a Reissue out of the Custom Shop in the early eighties, I also recall someone telling me long ago of how Billy Gibbons of ZZ Top had a guitar collection that was unrivaled, and that he purportedly had an original Modern locked away, somewhere of suspect origin. This was all fine and dandy, and no doubt the stuff of urban legend, and I settled into the fact that Id never know, but it would be really cool one day to see one.

Flash forward 10 -15 years and we find ourselves with Mr. Gibbons releasing a book "Billy F. Gibbons - Rock and Roll Gear-head" telling the story of ZZ Top, his love of custom hot-rod cars, and showing off a selection of his prized collection of guitars. Imagine my glee when I found out that not only would I be able to attain a copy of this book, but the man himself would be at Indigo in the Eaton Center signing copies and making nice with the prolls.

While not a huge fan of ZZ Top's catalogue, I did recall that one of the first couple of 45's I bought as a young teen was Sleeping Bag (loved that guitar) and I totally do appreciate what the man has done in the field of collecting and using rare fine odd shaped instruments, something I dabble in as well. (I have an Explorer and several V's -still waiting for my Moderne). So I queued up and waited my turn amongst a strange assortment of folk, old and young that had turned up to get a copy, get it signed, and meet something of a rock and roll legend, in tow, all the crazy crap that they brought for him to sign, including, I-kid-you-not, the dash of a Model A Ford.

After a lengthy wait, I finally got to the front, and the poor man, a consummate gentleman I might add, was frantically signing and meeting people as fast he could as his handlers had booked him for an interview at a local radio station and time was fast running out with lines still long. Far gone were the notions of posed photos, personalized messages and long chats with the man, and people were getting hurried through.

What follows was my interaction with the man himself (my Memorex here is my head, so apologies if I don't get the exact details right).

[handler one] Next
[jef] Its a pleasure to meet you
[BFG] Why, thank you.
[jef] So. Do you really own an original Moderne?
[BFG] We don't know (adjusts sunglasses). They cant tell me.
It came out of San Antonio, its dated from the late 50's (signs my book).
[security guard] Please move along sir.
[BFG] I bought it from a house painter they never...
[Security guard] please sir, move over here.
[handler two] you'll have to move over here sir
[jef] sorry,.thank you!

He kept talking to me, telling me the story of the research that they have done into the Moderne shaped instrument that he owns, but (I think) effectively has not been able to substantiate officially as one of the prototypes, but I was shuffled off to the side, and while I was busy respecting authority, I ended up missing the last half of the tale. He was very polite and friendly, and seemed engaged by the question.

Dan Erlewine's Moderne

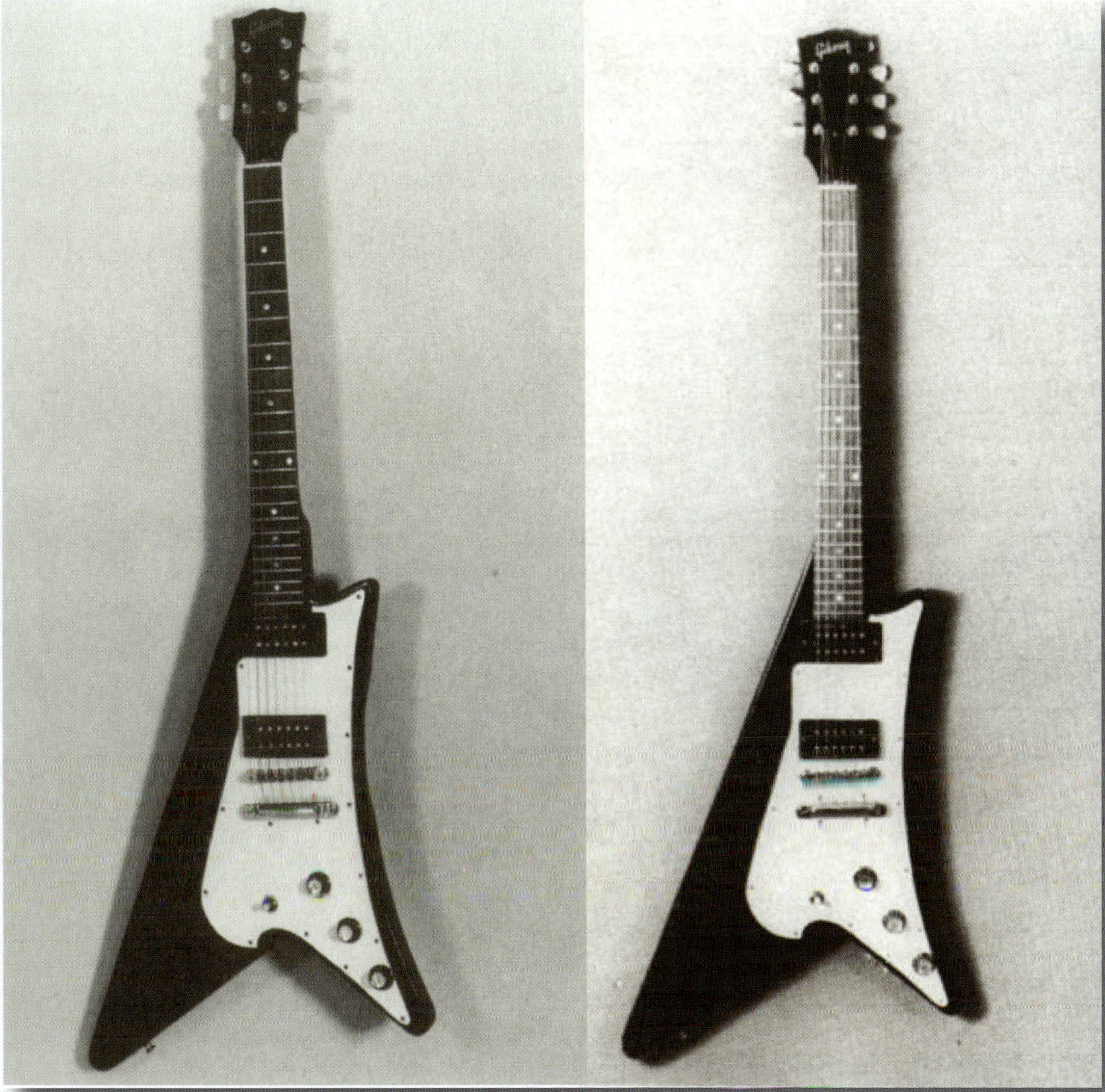

I interviewed Dan over the phone about this particular guitar.This is what he remembers:" I did have a Moderne for a short while. It belonged to a man in Detroit. He had taken it back to Gibson at some point and had a Melody Maker neck put on it because he liked his buddy's Melody Maker neck better. I bought it thinking that it was an Explorer which I had never seen either. This was in the days when you never checked anything before buying it or else didn't want to spoil the deal by messing around and waiting. You snatched fast."

"I only owned the guitar for a few days. The guy that sold it to me was the original owner, old enough to be legit. I took off the pickguard and found secondary routing underneath. I realized it wasn't 'original'. I made a few fast VERY strange attempts to patch up the unwanted pickup holes fast and finish over them. I hadn't the time or desire to fill the holes with wood, and at that time I didn't have a milling machine to help me do it well. $175 would have broken me. I had to sell it ASAP. I may have (of all things) filled the holes with Plaster Of Paris. It couldn't have lasted long, for sure. I had never used "Bondo" at that point, nor did I have an industrial epoxy that might have worked. After I had repaired it, I quickly sold it for the same $175 that I paid for it. I sold it to the Ann Arbor Music Mart and they put it in the window. Soon, George Gruhn's manager Doug Green came walking along. Doug was in town visiting. (This is now 'Ranger Doug' of Grand Old Opry fame). Doug saw it, called George and described it and they concluded that it was a moderne. Doug bought it instantly for $1000. Later, George was ticked when he found the same things I had found but Ann Arbor Music Mart plead 'Caveat Emptor'. This was early 1970's. It was a moderne body, and a real Gibson. The owner was just a normal guy, not a hustler, just a guy that wanted a quick $175. Think what you like, but it was a genuine Moderne. I wish I had taken pictures of it. The guitar was real but had been messed with. The previous owner said he had sent it back to the factory and had a Melody Maker neck installed on it. This was WAY before people were lying and faking stuff. The photo in Tom Wheeler's book is the very guitar that I'm talking about. The man I bought it from was a regular, normal, person - not a big time musician, just an ordinary bloke. Sincere, honest, and believable. So the guitar in Wheeler's book is not a 'fake' at all. A Gibson Moderne with a Melody Maker neck put on it, and some other weird stuff going on with the pickups just like amateur guitar butchers used to do back then. At the time I thought it was an Explorer. I hadn't seen one of them yet. I sold it to the Ann Arbor Music Mart as an Explorer. They put it in the window as an Explorer. Doug Green walked by and thought it was a Moderne. Plus, in a way he was correct."

Dan Erlewine's Moderne backup story from Robb Lawrence:

While visiting Gibson and Ann Arbor in 1972, some very knowledgeable local guitar guys told me about that very Moderne guitar in black. They played the guitar a few times and described it as having the Gumby headstock and biggest neck they had ever played! This all happened before the Detroit fellow unfortunately had Gibson re-neck it. That Louisville slugger must have been as big or bigger than most Explorers.

A few years later when Gruhn told me that he had a black Moderne with an odd neck, I instantly thought of the one I'd heard about but didn't put two and two together at the time. I thought someone had seen that black one and made a cheap copy. I personally believe Dan actually had this very guitar from his description here. Maybe it was painted black due to the streaks of dark coloration Korina sometimes has.

During my interviews at Bigsby with Ted McCarty in '72, he discussed the three guitars and showed me his design patents. I mentioned I had seen a few Explorers and Flying Vs but never the rare "Sailfin" guitar. Ted said they made a few Modernes but didn't know what had happened to them. He added that many prototypes of various guitars were destroyed. I know they sometimes were bought by employees such as the 1951 sharp cutaway Les Paul solidbody I found in Kalamazoo that year. Therefore this modified black Moderne is quite the Rarebird of solidbody Gibsons.

I did hear of another natural one up in the Northwest that is under complete wraps. The lady and her husband know exactly what it is and are totally hush about it. No pictures or articles whatsoever. If that's on the level, maybe it will surface someday as the real "Holy Grail"! Speaking of the Reverend's Sailfin; Billy Gibbons once showed me a black and white photo of his Moderne guitar at a concert. It was on a proof sheet and was very hard to see clearly. He invited me to play it in Houston sometime. Billy said he wasn't sure what to think of it. Someday I'll get a gander at it.

Billy Gibbons Choice Collection

© May, 1984 Guitar World reprinted with permission

Besides being an avid collector (he owns, at last count, some two hundred-seventy guitars, many of which are securely locked in vaults), Billy Gibbons is also a designer of guitar shapes. He currently holds nine patents and has a couple pending. His designs are being distributed through the Hondo line and the Dean line.Gibbons' interest in designing guitar shapes dates back to his years as an art school student at the University of Texas. He adds, "Of course, my studies fell by the wayside as soon as music started kicking in. The Moving Sidewalks had released a couple of records that started getting notoriety, so I then decided to make music a full-time endeavor. But not wanting to get too far away from my art school background, I've kept up my interest in design as well."

Photos©Rob McElyea

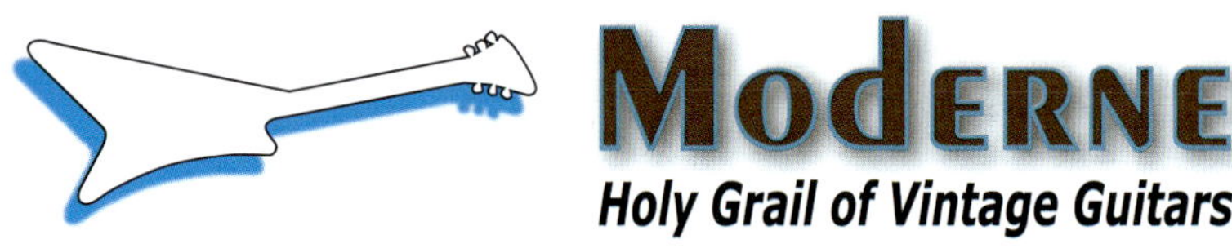

Perhaps one of his rarest items is a '57 or '58 Gibson Moderne, which he purchased in San Antonio in 1971. This particular guitar has achieved mythic status over the years. Some say it doesn't exist. Others insist it's the rare bird that all collectors dream of, the unicorn of collectibles.

Billy explains: "In 1957, Gibson introduced three new guitars-the Explorer, the Flying V and the Moderne. The only two to make it to the Chicago convention were the Flying V and the Explorer. Apparently, they decided to pull the Moderne. Rumor has it that about fifty of them were manufactured, but the records at Gibson are so sketchy that they're unable to confirm their whereabouts or their authenticity without actually seeing the instruments." He says his Moderne is not in pristine condition but is still very playable. "And it's kind of amusing," he adds. "When I bring it up out of the vaulty, people think it looks like a sailfish. In fact, we used to call it The Sailfish." He had heard stories about his legendary instrument before he actually came across one. "Finally, I contacted a guy who had one. He was a player but he really didn't like the guitar because it was unlike anything that was popular at the time. And I tellya, it's unlike anything that's popular now. But I bought it for a little bit of nothing. It had Gibson written at the top of the neck and it had two humbucking pickups. That was enough for me. I remember telling the guy, 'Well, it looks like a warclub, but I'll take it.' There's no serial number on it. The finish is still intact ... a Korina body with a clear finish, same as the V and the Explorer. And it's got a pickguard but it doesn't have fastening screws. It was just glued onto the body. It remains just as I found it. It had been unaltered except for being smashed on. Whoever was playing it certainly was proud of an E7th chord."

As for its authenticity, Billy admits he has some doubts himself. "We've really never been able to get any solid verification from Gibson. A couple of reps have seen it, but they're too young to have been around when it was made. So far, it's just never been seen by any of those Gibson people who were around in '57." But despite any possible doubts, he is quick to add, "I'm a big fan of this Moderne cult and I claim to have a very sharp eye on these matters of identification. And there are certain things about this guitar that might indicate it is the real thing ... the shape of the pickup, the holes, the workmanship of the routing, the fingerboard, the frets, the neck width. All these things indicate that it's an older vintage. So although I can't absolutely prove its authenticity as yet, I have every reason to believe it is a very rare instrument. I'm proud to own it."

Photo © Bob Alford

Billy Gibbons' Moderne

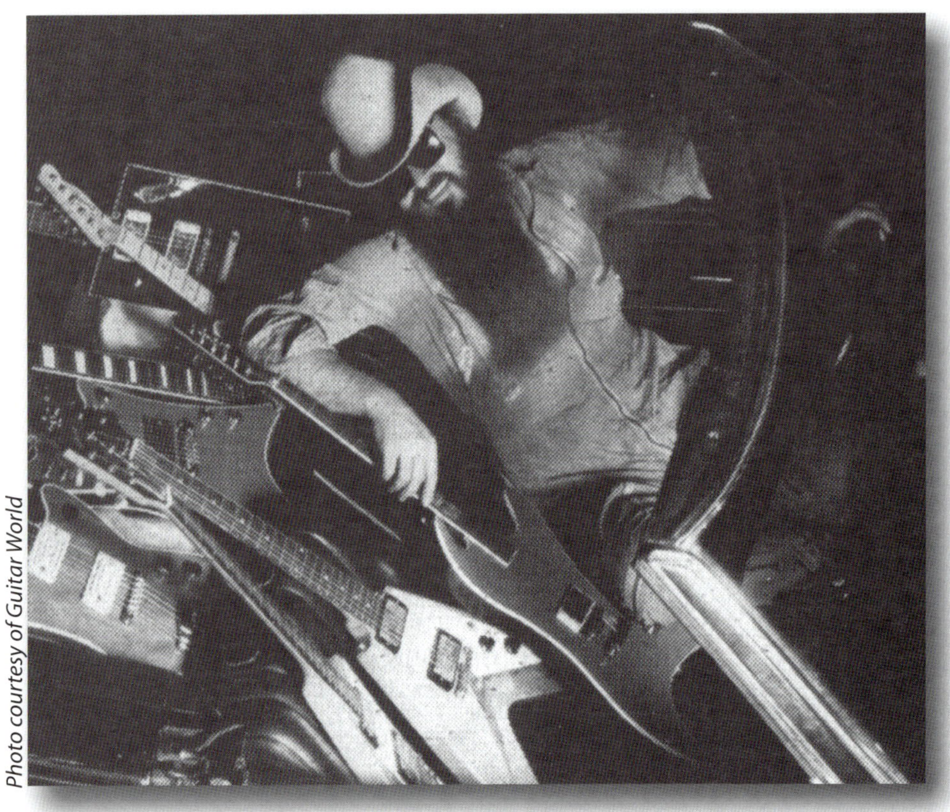

Photo courtesy of Guitar World

In this photo, you can see Billy's Moderne peeking out from behind the Flying V.

Seymour Duncan has seen Billy's Moderne and he thinks it is a real Gibson based on what he knows. He said that it was beat up and ugly - looked like a rough prototype or something. Seymour said this in the mid '80's. The suggestion was made that Billy's Moderne was so beat up that Billy didn't want to show it off and have the "Moderne Mystique and Mojo" ruined.

Numerous attempts were made by the author over a one year period to get an interview from Mr. Gibbons. He didn't respond.

Chapter 9
Interviews

Howard Leese and his Quest for the Moderne

by Cohn Rude
reprinted with permission

The band Heart sports one of the finest guitar players I have encountered. Not only is his music terrific, but he has been a well known Gibson collector for many years. In talking with Howard at the Seattle Guitar show he agreed to bring his prototype mahogany moderne to the Portland Guitar Show on May 22nd to do an interview about his long pursuit of the original 1958 moderne. In retrospect I'm glad we agreed on the Portland Show to do the interview. Not only was Howard's prototype there, but in addition, there was an F series Moderne, one, non-original Futura and the first Korina wood prototype Moderne.

Howard when did you first try to acquire an original moderne?

In 1984 Heart was moving through its tour schedule when one of our concert stops was Mexico City. Prior to the performance that night I received a call from a gentleman that said he had an original 1958 moderne which he wanted to sell. The asking price was $50,000. I informed him the price was acceptable I would get an international money order to pay for it. I was told that the guitar was black in color and that it might possibly have been in a fire. I didn't have him go into extensive details on the phone assuming that he would bring it over that night. We agree to meet at my hotel room after the performance. Unfortunately he never showed up with the Moderne.

Howard what about Billy Gibbons' Moderne?

I recently asked Billy Gibbons about his Instrument he informed me it is Korina wood with all the correct hardware, the only anomaly is the Les Paul head stock. Billy showed it to Gibson and they said it was Authentic. Billy himself believes it to be real.

Howard, what other solid proof do you have of the existence of a 1958 Moderne?

I approached Ted McCarty at the NAMM show in 1993. In 1958 he was in upper management with Gibson. Ted himself was involved in development and design of this guitar. He told me that 6 Modernes were completed and because they didn't sell they went to guys in the factory.

Howard tell us about your prototype Moderne.

In early 1982, Gibson made 6 mahogany prototype Modernes which runs parlay to 1958 when they also used mahogany on all modernistic prototypes before they went to the Korina wood runs.

Interesting point that Ted McCarty said 6 1958 Modernes were made and in 1982 Gibson made 6 prototypes. The guitar I have is candy apple red in color with the black white black small pick guard. It has all gold hardware 24 3/4 scale. Identical other than wood to the 1983 Korina wood production run Modernes.

Right: Howard Leese's prototype Gibson Moderne A-001.

Walter Carter

Have you ever heard Gibson employees in Kalamazoo named Frank D'Angelo or Reno Alberti?

Haven't heard of either of those guys.

Is it possible for Gibson to make a prototype of a guitar with the intent to have it in production even though no case was made for the guitar?

Gibson would make the prototype and then send it out for a case fitting. It's conceivable that there could be a delay on the part of the case company and that the guitars could be in production before the cases were ready. Anything's possible with Gibson, of course.

The Flying V was listed in Gibson's shipping records as "Flying V gtr." correct? Was there any entry with the name of Explorer or Futura?

The V is listed on production totals as Flying "V". The other listing is Korina (Mod. Gtr). I don't have a copy of Larry Meiners' Flying V book handy, but he has a photo of a page from the shipping ledger. I think it's just "Flying V." There is no mention anywhere of Explorer or Futura. Meiners got his copy of the Gibson ledger page from me, but I'm not sure I can locate it now.

What and where are the Gibson Archives and who can access them?

The archives are at Gibson in various places but mostly in the customer service and marketing areas. There's no one at Gibson now who can help with historical stuff now.

Have you ever heard of a vintage guitar collector named Cynthia Zander and or David Revell?

Never heard of Zander or Revell. They haven't done any business with Gruhn Guitars since we started using computers in 1997.

Did Gibson ever sell prototypes to the public or were they ever passed on to dealers or sales people?

Gibson would sell anything, especially in hard times. In the 1980's a lot of guitars were stamped Custom Shop Prototype, but they were mostly just limited or "exploratory" runs. Real prototypes weren't labeled as such.

Do you know what Gibson's policy on employee purchases was in the late 50's?

Don't know about employee purchases in the late 1950's.

Did Gibson ever make a 50's left handed korina Flying V?

Can't remember if I've seen a lefty V or not. I don't think so.

When Gibson closed the kalamazoo plant, did they auction a lot of stuff off? Was the general public able to get that stuff? Did they have an inventory of any of it?

When Kalamazoo closed they sent everything useful to Nashville. Some of the employees may have bought some of the equipment. The collection of Orville Gibson instruments was left there, I believe, until Henry J. bought Gibson in 1986. There may have been a few other things. I've never heard of an auction.

Do you know how to get in contact with a fella named Billy Gibbons? I really would like to interview him for this book but being new to all this, I don't know how to go about it. I know he did a foreword for a book by Larry Meiners but Larry's email does not work at the moment. I think he might be interested in my book as well.

Here's an address for Z.Z. Top's management office: 5757 Westheimer #3139, Houston, TX 77057. It may be old.

Cohn Rude

If you don't mind, I'd like to ask you a couple questions about what you wrote in your article in Vintage Guitar Magazine.

Yeah, no problem, no problem.

You said you found some pictures of a...there was some templates in the pictures

Well...yeah...at the Gibson factory you can see the templates in there... and...it's been a while since I...I'd have to read it again but i think if I recall there's a Flying V template and a Moderne template was in there. I'm pretty sure. I'd have to re-look at that stuff.

Where did you see that from?

Well...you know I think that's in Tom Wheeler's book, if I'm not mistaken.

Which one, American Guitars?

Yeah, I think it's American Guitars. I think that's where I found it. But, as it turns out, um...I spent 25 years tracking that guitar down, following every lead, um..there was only one that was real. The others had been build outside the factory. The one that's real Billy Gibbons owns it.

Now, I heard that rumor too, and I talked to George Gruhn about it and he said that he's known Billy for years and that Billy has never brought it up. Now, another guy, when Billy was doing a book signing for his book he just came out with...one of the guys that was getting his book signed asked him about it and he started to talk about it but he didn't have enough time to finish cos they were like you know, pushing people through the line real quick.

They published a picture of that in Guitar World.

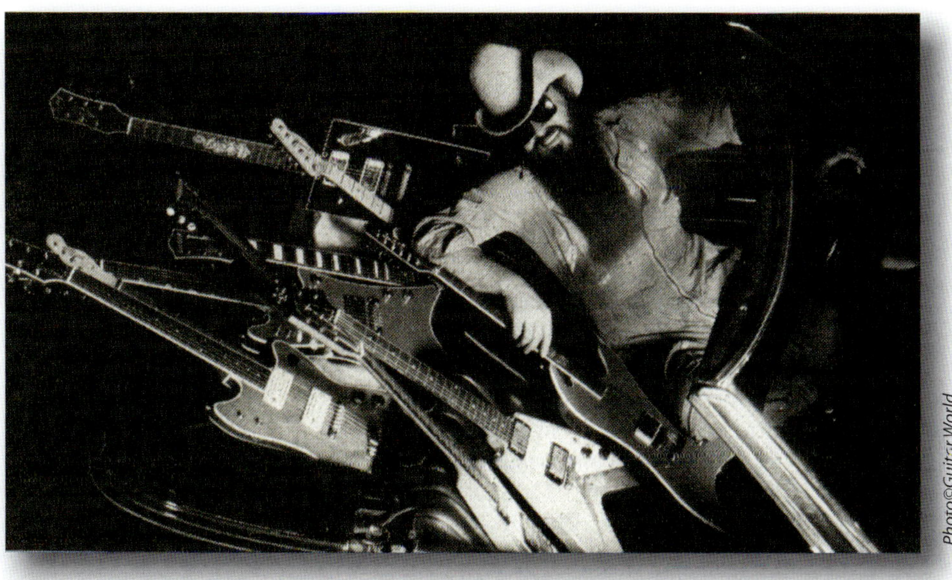

Photo©Guitar World

I spent...I spent more time on finding that guitar, tracking that guitar than he could ever dream of. And I tracked down every one of the ones that were supposed to be real and the only one that's real is Billy Gibbons'...and ...um...I've also got....there was one knockoff you can use the pictures if you want...made in California and shipped up to Oregon an exact replica of Billy Gibbons'... but that's the guitar. It's got a glued on pickguard ...there were several Futura's that were made in the factory but only one Moderne. I've talked to Billy in person...last time he came through town he gave me $180 worth of concert tickets and he's a nice guy, he's a regular guy. He's had the guitar for years. There's also a story about that Erlewine made that guitar but he did not make Gibbons' guitar... But I don't know that Billy will let you have pictures. He's pretty secretive about it... he doesn't ya know.... he showed it to Gibson, he showed it to Gibson reps and Gibson reps said it looked right to them and then I kinda finished with the research on the guitar. But anyway...it is published in Guitar World.

(After Cohn had sent me a box of information he had collected about the Modernistic Guitars, I called him back.)

That was some really good reading.

Well that was like 25 years of my life in that little box(laughs).

Just like you predicted, I have questions...first question is...this guy Tony. Who is Tony and how does he know so much about this stuff?

Tony was a guy who contacted me after I published my article "Moderne: Fact or Fiction" and started supplying me with information that he said he was getting from driving around the country trying to find these Moderne guitars. So that's who he was. I never actually met him and I don't have a phone number for him now. But that was Tony.

In some of those letters there is one where he mentions sending you a photograph of something...did he ever send you pictures of guitars that he saw?

He never sent me a picture of a Moderne. Never. You know we can never really be sure if Tony was on the up and up or not.

He just contacted you out of nowhere like I did?

Yeah he contacted me because I was publishing the article and he looked me up and I think he was trying to find the Moderne, was very interested. The only credible thing was he claims he went to Cynthia Zander's house who had the Moderne that died and we actually tracked down that yes she did have the Moderne...but the one that she had was built by the guy that worked at the Gibson factory building his house, the friend of Ted McCarty, which I'd have to look the name up but yeah.

So she died...does anybody know what happened to the guitar after that?

Yeah um, the guitar is still around but it wasn't built at the Gibson factory. It was built...I'd have to pull the book out and look at that stuff again...but it was built by a friend of Ted McCarty's that worked for Gibson and it was built in his house. So the guitar is still floating around but the guy George Manno...do you remember reading anything about that?

Yeah.

George Manno might be able to get someone to connect with that guitar but again, not a built in the Gibson factory guitar.

So how does this George Manno fit into everything?

George Manno says he knew Tony and he said Tony was a little flaky but he knew Tony. George Manno was a violin repair man and builder in Chicago. But that where he ties in.

So he knew this Tony guy?

He knew Tony and he knew the guy that built the guitars in his house that worked with Ted McCarty at Gibson. So he's kind of a good source George Manno is.

Did you ever find out any more about Mrs. Lacomi? She was the wife of the guy that supposedly built these copies? He worked at Gibson and didn't work there very long and he supposedly took some stuff with him when he left.

That would be the guy...Alberti Reno...Reno Alberti I believe is who you are talking about there. He's the guy that built the guitar that was in Tom Wheeler's book and some others. He took the drawings home for the Modernistic guitars.

I was going over some of these notes and one of the questions I have is if you followed up on any of these names that Tony wrote about, all these different names that are in there, Cynthia Zander?

Cynthia Zander that was followed up on cos she actually, there was a blurb published on her in 20th Century Guitar when she had passed away. That guitar was the only one that we were ever really able to verify existed. So Cynthia, yeah, she was followed up on.

What do you mean "verified"?

The guitar was built but it was built by the friend of Ted McCarty at his house along with some other stuff....an Explorer....several other guitars that were built. Frank D'Angelo was the guy that built the guitar. He was the friend of Ted McCarty's. Frank D'Angelo is the guy that built the guitar that Cynthia Zander had. Tony actually saw that guitar but it wasn't built in the Gibson factory. And then the other guy, Reno Alberti, he's the guy that went to work for Harmony and he's the one that built the Moderne that's in Tom Wheeler's book American Guitars published years ago that they said was a fake. Reno Alberi built that guitar and another one. Reno Alberti left Gibson, took a lot of the prototype drawings of the Modernistic guitars and went to work for Harmony and was with them for a number of years.

I think some of that stuff was made up by Tony because he said he found a guitar in Oregon, ya know he found all these guitars that just didn't make sense, I mean we'd never heard of any of these pieces so that was the problem with Tony.

Both Frank D'Angelo and Reno Alberti worked for Gibson at one time. Frank D'Angelo was the friend of Ted McCarty's and built several guitars in his house and his daughter still has some of those guitars.

Who's daughter does?

Frank D'Angelo daughter.

Do you know her name?

George Manno has that information.

But this Tony guy never took pictures of that guitar when he saw it?

No, he never took pictures of the guitar.

Have you ever seen any pictures of any of those guitars other than the Wheeler one?

The daughter of Frank D'Angelo brought in some of the guitars to George Manno's shop. One was an Explorer. So George has actually seen the pieces. Whether he photographed them that I don't know.

So you think a lot of this Tony stuff is made up?

I think a lot of it we just couldn't really verify was the problem. He was Moderne crazy. We just couldn't prove, other than the one guitar Cynthia Zander's was the only one we could prove.

What about that guitar Billy Gibbons has?

That guitar is what we believe is the real Moderne and we believe it was built in the Gibson factory. I talked to Billy about it for about 30 minutes. He wanted to know about the article I published, he wanted to know about his guitar and I told him after all my years of research that he had the real Moderne that was built in the factory. We had a good talk. I should have pushed a little harder to get pictures of it then from him. I haven't talked to him in 11 years now. I think that once he understands (about your book) that he would want to share it with the guitar community.

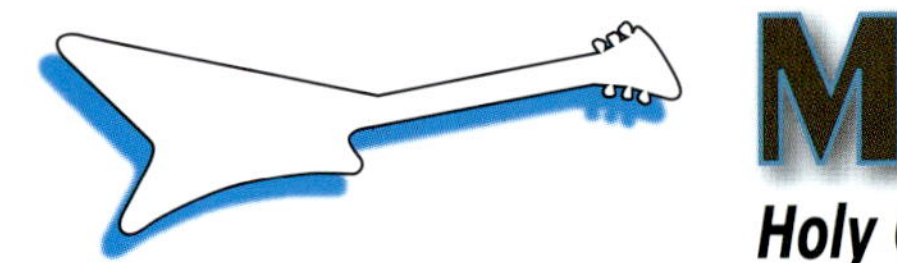

Scott Matteson

Do you know Cohn Rude?

Yeah Cohn, yeah. He's the guy that tried to write an article or something like that(about the Moderne). Cohn was going to have a whole article on my guitar printed in the Vintage Guitar Magazine and they wouldn't put it in the magazine.

Why not?

Because they are afraid it's not real. See that's the problem when you run into these prototypes is are they real, are they not? A lot of people won't bring out rare guitars because of that.

The Moderne situation...here's what I know. I had a guy, an old man come in my shop and he had a brown '50's case, like the ' 58 V's have...kinda of triangulated and I opened it up and it was pink inside and you could see they very clear impression of a Moderne body.

How long ago was that?

Probably about eight years ago (1999).

I tried to question the guy and he wouldn't tell me anything. He told me he just bought the case from somebody. But somewhere there was a guitar (to go with the case). He wouldn't give me any information whatsoever but I saw it myself and I know damn good and well there's Modernes out there.

Scott Matteson's 1955 Explorer prototype

You say "Modernes" as in plural.

Yeah I think there's three of them out there somewhere. Billy Gibbons supposedly has one I don't know what the story is on that. I saw a picture that he allowed taken where he was standing, he had three guitars and they were sitting kinda sideways so the picture was kinda sideways but you could see the Korina wood and you could sorta see the body but not very clearly.

It's time these guitars got out there to be seen. This is a long road that everybody's been on. I know besides Cohn there's been other people that have tried to run down this road and it's just really difficult so I'm glad you're doing it and glad you're getting a book together for it cos it deserves to be brought to light.

Supposedly from what Cohn and I heard is that there is one with the Les Paul headstock, one with a split V headstock, and one with the paddle stick headstock.

I worked for Gibson twice, once when I was young and that's when Stan who was the wood buyer worked there. Then I worked for them for eight years back in the '90's. I originally worked for the Kalamazoo factory and that was just about the time that they sold it or was getting out of there to go to Nashville. I worked down here doing some prototypying, I did some finish work, repair work...a lot of hard core stuff that they didn't want to have to send back to Nashville, I did. I was given a 100% capabilities so I could do finishes and all kinds of stuff. So, ya know, I worked at a pretty high level and I was in touch with a lot of these people.

Wanna take me as an apprentice? (laughs)

I built a lot of replicas. There's a lot of replicas out there that I built. Gibson actually allowed me to build their replicas for the Scorpions. So I built Rudolph's V's, I built Matthias some Explorers in Korina wood.

So there is a case out there somewhere.

There was a case. Some old guy had it. You could see the indentation (of the Moderne) just as clear as day. So there might have been one (an original Moderne) in San Diego but at this point, who knows?

And he was trying to sell you the case or just wanted your opinion on it?

I don't know what he was trying to do.

He just brought the case in and showed you?

Yeah...and I tried to find out everything I could and he just wouldn't budge. But I guarantee you...I guarantee you I saw it.

You didn't take any picture of it by any chance did you?

No I sure didn't. When I saw it I was trippin out...I wanted to find out where the guitar was. The case was in beautiful shape, almost mint.

How old do you think the guy was?

Oh he was in his probably 70's. Late 60's early 70's.

And this happened in San Diego?

Yeah. That showed me that there definitely is one out there. At least one. I suspect and I talked to Gibson about it and the prototypes they built in the mid fifties for these guitars were all done out of Mahogany and then they decided to build them out of Korina wood after that. So all of the prototypes that were built, were built out of Mahogany, so there is probably a Mahogany Moderne out there.

Yeah I figured if I can pass information on to you I would love to get all the information you can that way...cos you're going to get people questioning things and stuff and you want to have the facts to back it up. All of those '50's prototype guitars are made out of one piece... other than the '58 V's. So the Moderne would probably be one piece.

One piece neck too?

Yeah. I've built some Modernes.

You did!

Yeah I built them with a split headstock. Two piece body and a split V headstock, those are the one's I built.

I've never seen any of those. Who'd you build them for?

Just general sales.

These were finished guitars?

Yeah. When I was working for Gibson, they basically allowed me to prototype and do stuff. I had permission from Gibson to do that. Some went to Japan. I probably built a hundred of them, V's, Explorers, and Modernes.

How many Modernes do you think you made?

Not too many of them...probably three or four.

And they all had the split headstock or did you experiment?

No, I just did the split headstock cos I thought it looked the best. They were all made from Korina wood. And the bodies are all two piece. I didn't have pieces big enough for a one piece body. The necks are one piece. You can always tell a fake by the fact that it will have a two piece body.

Photo©Rick Gould

Howard Leese

Hello Howard. I am publishing a book about the Moderne and I was wondering if you would like to talk about it?

yeah yeah. You're doing a book about the Moderne?

Yes I am. It's almost finished.

Really?

Cohn Rude and I have been talking a lot about it and he sent me a bunch of stuff he had collected over the years and some of his articles he has given me permission to reprint. There is an interview he did with you a few years back and you got some prototypes of the Heritage series reissues and I was wondering if you might want to talk about some of that?

Yeah I did have a prototype of the reissues ones but um...what's your take on weather they built any real ones back in the day?

I say yes. And I think that Billy Gibbons has one and I think the one Dan Erlewine had was original.

yeah?

Cos I was gonna say that Billy's... Billy says he's got one and Gibson has looked at it and they think it's real. That's about the closest that I know of one actually existing. I heard of another one that was in Mexico City years ago...a black one that had been in a fire but was still in one piece but I researched it a little bit but was never able to get a picture. I heard that story that the employees took a couple of them out because they were not going to go into production and I also heard that they took a couple of them and put them on the bandsaw and chopped them up into pieces.

I think six got made.

I've heard six, I've heard twelve, I've heard two. It's hard to say...those records are so vague and there doesn't seem like anyone has a definitive testimony about it. I met Ted McCarty and asked him about it you know and he was pretty old by then.

On the Heritage Modernes...how did you get involved with that?

What happened was when they started re-doing those in 82, I had a prototype Flying V, an "A" series Flying V and I liked that a lot...I thought that was a cool guitar and so I called Gibson because I heard that they were going to make Modernes and I talked to somebody there and he goes "yeah we are, were going to make them and we are just about to make the prototypes and I said ok well I want to buy two of the prototypes cos they made six and they were not Korina, they were Mahogany. Far as I know all six were Mahogany. The two I had were Mahogany for sure. I asked them(Gibson) to paint them Candy Apple red. I got the guitars, I got one for me and one for my tech at the time and I told him to do what I was going to do was put it away, don't even open the case, just put it away for a number of years which we did. Then we did a trade for them at some point and got some old Marshall gear for it at some point but I paid $500 a piece for them and got $5000 a piece for them. As far as I know, they were the only two red ones and they were Mahogany.

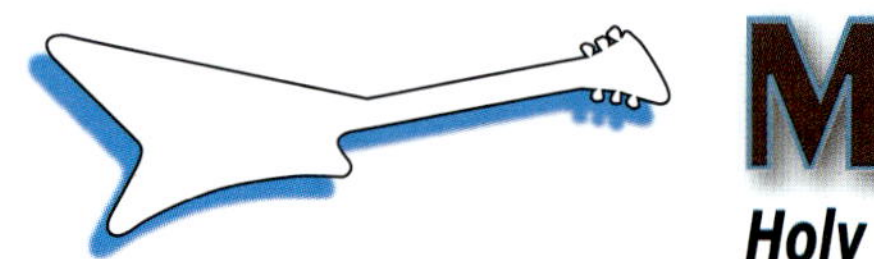

Do you remember who you called at Gibson

No but I just called Gibson cos I had been an endorsee since the 70's and I asked them about it and they said yeah we are making them.

Have you always been into the Moderne?

Well...yeah, I mean I like all of those. I like the Explorer , I like the Futura, the V and I thought all those guitars were really great and the Moderne was more of a legend than anything else so when they said well yeah were gonna make them and they are gonna be reissues but at least they'll be real Gibson Moderne's, I thought well that's great!

Had you heard of the Moderne before that?

Sure.

I was gonna steer you to Billy because I know, I think he has one.

I have pictures of Billy's Moderne, I've talked to his publicist, I've called everybody and their brother to try to get the word over to him I'd really like to talk to him about that guitar and I just think it's a lost cause by now.

You just haven't had the right guy call (laughs).

Cohn said he knew him and...

Yeah...Cohn is not a fellow rock star though.

You've actually talked to Billy about his huh...have you ever seen it?

No, I've never seen it but I asked him about it and he goes(does a Billy Gibbons impression)"Well...yes I do have one" he goes..."I think it's real...Gibson thinks it's real...everyone else can think what they like" (laughs)

Well the pictures I have it's a full on shot of the guitar but it's a black and white and you can't really make out any detail.

I think maybe by keeping it hidden, it keeps it mysterious plus you kinda don't want to advertise the fact that you have a guitar that's probably worth like ten million bucks or whatever it is.

Well all his guitars are worth a lot of money (laughs).

You don't have any Moderne's now?

No, I do not unfortunately.

Do you still have an interest in them?

Oh yeah.

So what is your belief on the originals, do you think any got made?

I do. I think there's a couple of them, like you said, I mean, they made the Futura, the V, and the Moderne and they didn't like...the only one they liked was the V. That's the only one that saw production...so they changed the Futura and turned it into the Explorer but the Futura never saw production and the Moderne never saw production but they had to have made a couple prototypes you know...it's just the way you do things.

Ted McCarty said in an interview that they never made just one of anything when they were starting projects like that.

Right. I've heard him say he thinks they made about twelve of them, but, who knows? I think it's interesting that the prototypes were Mahogany as opposed to Korina and then when they reissued them the prototypes again were Mahogany.

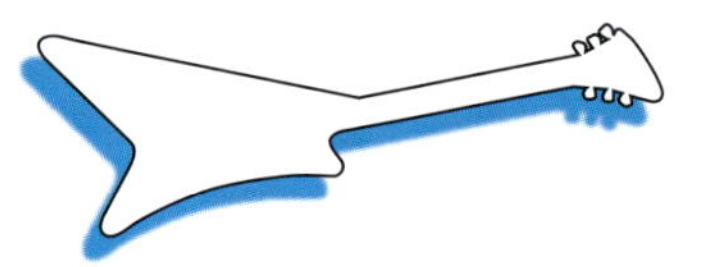

So tell me about the Moderne in Mexico City.

Somebody said I can get this guitar and are you interested in buying it and so I said yeah and I said let me see some pictures before we get too serious and if I like the way the pictures look I'll fly down there and look at it. They described it and it was painted black and it was a little crispy from being in a fire a little bit of damage but it was fine.

Did they say if it had a "Gumby" headstock or a Les Paul headstock?

A "Gumby" headstock I believe.

Did they say if it had a big pickguard or a little pickguard?

No, I didn't get that far on it. They just told me it was painted black.

Ok well...let me see if I can help you with Billy otherwise good luck on your project and send me a copy when you are done.

I appreciate you talking to me.

©Cohn Rude

Howard Leese Prototype
Moderne A-001

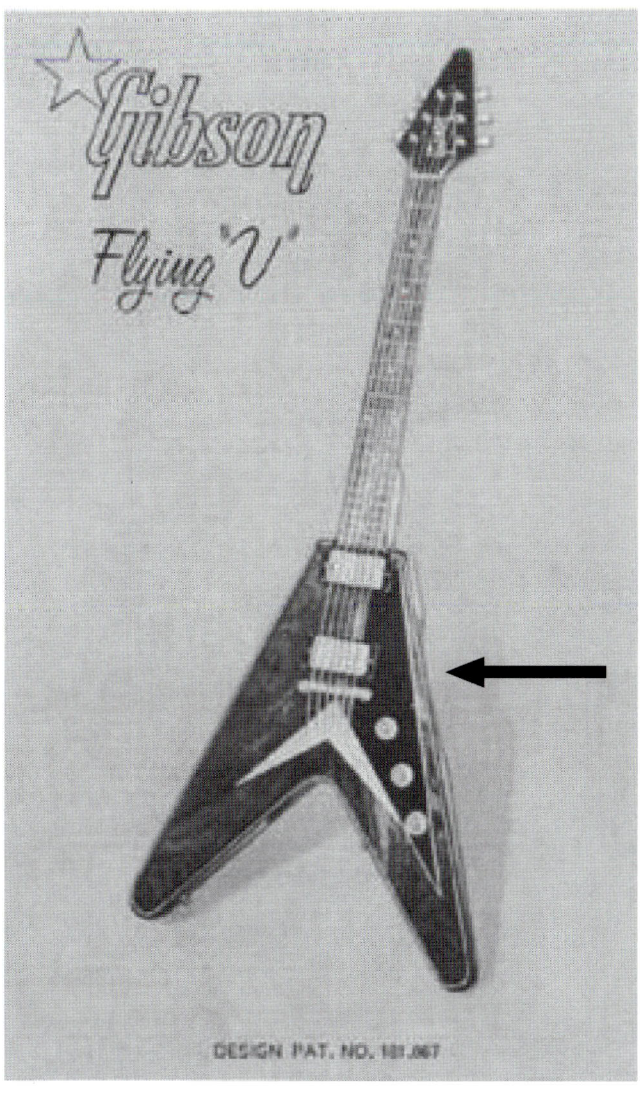

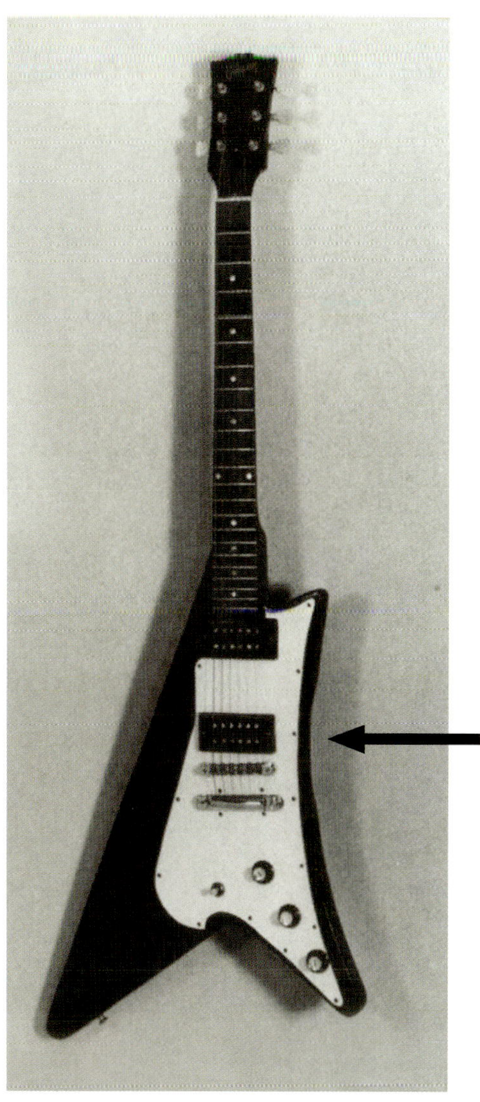

The Flying V from the Gibson Gazette, which was most likely a prototype, has a relief carved in the bottom of the body. You can see from the picture of the Moderne that it too has this same relief carved into the bottom part of the guitar.

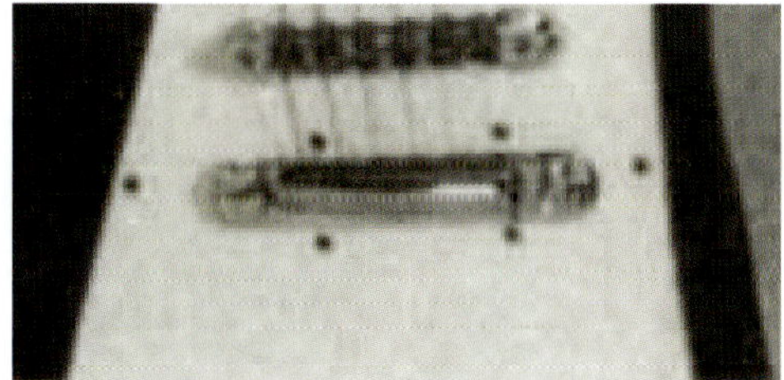

Another strange feature on this Moderne is the four screws attached to the pickguard above and below the tailpiece.

What Does George Gruhn Think?

Do you think an original Gibson Moderne exists?

I have never seen an original Moderne, but I've certainly seen plenty of obvious fakes. I have been told about some supposed originals, but none of these people ever as much sent me a photo. I'll believe it when I see it, but certainly not until. So far as I'm concerned, if there were any quantity of original Modernes, one should have surfaced by now. In the case of 12 fret prewar D-45 Martins, for example, only three appear on the company records, and I know where all three of them are. Other extremely rare models seem to show upon the market when the price warrants bringing them out of hiding. The fact that no credible instance of a Moderne has turned up leads me to think that there are none out there. Certainly, if one were to appear I would want to very carefully examine it. The incentive for a skilled forger to make one would be considerable. If a genuine original were indeed to appear many collectors would remain highly skeptical at least until it were very carefully examined by more than one highly qualified appraiser.

Of course what you sent me was your info about Billy Gibbons and his Moderne. This Billy and his Moderne thing is sort of an interesting story but as far as I know he's never been willing to show that guitar to anybody who actually knows guitars. If Billy really, really wanted to know if it was real he would have sent it up here, shown it to us. He's had it for years. There are numerous guitar specialists who Billy knows that he could have shown it to. It looks phoney as a three dollar bill in the photos.

What gives it away in the photos?

Well for one thing it's got a standard Gibson peghead shape which is highly unlikely. I have seen a couple of fakes that were early that had that feature. In fact, I had one of my employees almost buy one that was like that. The idea that the pickguard doesn't even have screws to fasten it is absurd. Gibson wouldn't do that not even on any prototype because when they made prototypes they still made them at the factory and they had access to all their equipment and they wouldn't do things as simple as not screw the pickguard on. The only "Moderne-ish" things I have seen that had that style standard Gibson peghead shape were obvious fakes.

Like the black one from Michigan(from Tom Wheeler's Book)?

There was a black one up there, yeah. It was old but not as old as a real Moderne and I think that this thing (Billy's Moderne) is something of that general ilk so it's not anything that would be collectable based on what I can see in those photos.

The main question *seems to be was any originals or prototypes made.*

Well, the simple fact is that no one seems to have a reliable answer. I have in my entire career never seen a Moderne that was real. In view of the fact that there are people who would pay half of a million dollars or more for one if you could prove it...if you could produce it...and it hasn't happened. I think that's a pretty good indication that if there ever was one, it's been destroyed.

Do you think that the Moderne like Billy has or the black one in Tom Wheeler's book...do you think its possible that there were left over bodies and parts laying around the plant and were taken and assembled outside of the plant?

That black one I had (the one in Tom Wheeler's book) was a crude piece of crap and I don't think it had anything to do with a Gibson Moderne that was made as a prototype. It had a Gibson neck stuck on it but it was a homemade body. My memories of it are from that period and even then it was crude to the point that it was obviously not real. It later ended up at Alex Music and they sold it for a fair amount of money to some dealer in Japan.

So far as what Billy has, I've seen that photo that you sent but that photo does nothing to convince me that it's real and makes me all the more of the opinion that it's not real. If Billy really truly wanted to find out, he would show it to people like me. He's known me since 1970. He knows darn well he could find out. He has chosen so far not to find out. So that's what I think.

Walter Carter: *I talked to Jim Durloo down at Heritage Guitars and he said they did what they call "soft tooling" prototypes of the Explorer and the Flying V so that they could tool up for them and they never did any soft tooling prototypes like that for the Moderne and additionally, he said there were racks in the hallway of Flying V's in the white and he never saw a rack with the Moderne.*

I think Julius Bellson kinda nodded when I asked him about it that there was a Moderne at the trade show. Ted McCarty said there was one at that trade show but Ted McCarty said there was never any solidbody Epiphone. I had the sheet where he had spec'd it out with his initials on the sheet for the solid body Epi's. The interview I did with Ted in 1993...I was doing the Gibson book and Tom Wheeler was contributing and I sent him my transcript of the interview with Ted just in case he wanted to use some of the quotes in his chapters, things I wasn't using. He said it was almost verbatim to the interview he had done with Ted for the American Guitars book which I think came out in 1984. So ten years had gone by and Ted had his stories down. I don't think he can be really counted on to have an accurate memory.

Well if Jim Durloo said there was nothing made...he was the guy who I thought would know for sure since he was there.

Yeah, he doesn't say "we absolutely didn't do it", but he says what he saw and that was none. He was involved in the tooling up for these things. So I would believe his story.

Tim Shaw

Tell me how you came to work for Gibson. What was your position? What helped you decide to work for Gibson?

I'd been working at a company called Sunrise Manufacturing in Kalamazoo; we made electric guitars and the Sunrise acoustic pickup. When that business began to fall apart in late 1975 I moved to the Bay Area in California. Shortly after, one of my partners in that business, Chuck Burge, was hired at Gibson by Bruce Bolen. Gibson was ramping up its R&D department. As that department grew, Chuck mentioned me to Bruce, and I was eventually hired by Gibson. It seemed too good an opportunity to pass up; I could be a repairman any time, but I figured I'd only have one shot at working for Gibson.

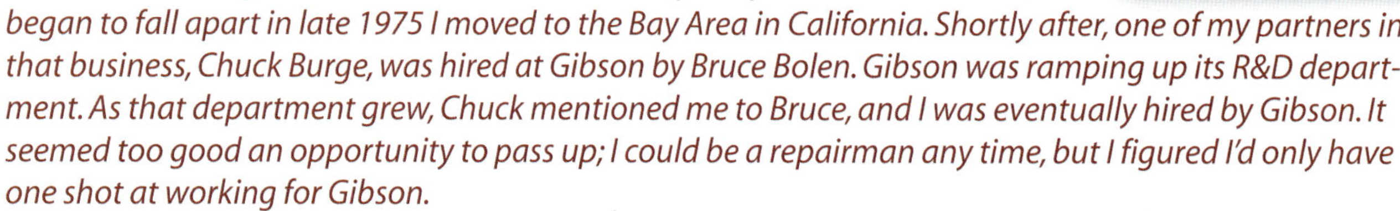

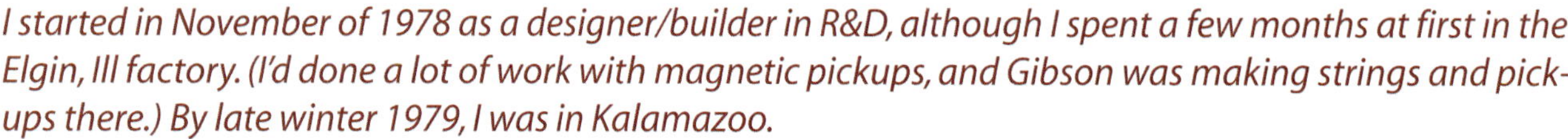

I started in November of 1978 as a designer/builder in R&D, although I spent a few months at first in the Elgin, Ill factory. (I'd done a lot of work with magnetic pickups, and Gibson was making strings and pickups there.) By late winter 1979, I was in Kalamazoo.

What prompted the Heritage Series reissues and why was the Moderne chosen for inclusion? Whose idea was it?

The Heritage series was developed by Bruce and the R&D staff, including Chuck, Abe Wechter, and me. We felt that there was a big gap between the classic Gibson designs and the way the current guitars were being made. I don't exactly consider the Moderne a Reissue in the same sense the Les Pauls were; the "Heritage Series" was two Les Pauls. However, we did start doing more solid body models as a result of that.

We'd had a mahogany Explorer since 1976, and we redid the Flying V in about 1981. The Moderne was added pretty late, since there was basically no information available about it.

When did you start working on the Heritage Series project?

It was introduced in 1980, as I recall.

What information was available to you for the specs of the Moderne other than the patent drawing?

Basically, nothing. Most Gibson drawings prior to about 1971 had been pitched years ago, so if there ever had been drawings of the Moderne we didn't have them.

Were the guitars done on CNC machines or more by hand(soft tooled)?

The earliest versions in Kalamazoo were made on pin routers and shapers; Kalamazoo didn't have CNC machinery. The tooling in Kalamazoo was first-rate for its time, and was pretty hard-tooled. However, there were many fixtures like the ones for pickup holes which could set up to run several different models.

Were any left handed models available of the Moderne?

Not that I remember.

Were custom colors available other than the Red prototypes? So far I know the colors available were: Black, White, Natural, and a small number of Red. Someone told me there was a matching Moderne and Explorer in Bahama Blue but I have not been able to verify that. Was a tobacco sunburst prototype made?

I don't recall a tobacco sunburst prototype, or any other colors. There were some blue ones; I remember selling a blue Moderne to John Sebastian after I moved to Nashville.

Did you talk to any of the old timers at Gibson about the possibility of an original for research purposes-(Ted McCarty, Julius Bellson, Jim Deurloo, Rem Wall, Stan Rendall,John Huis, Clarence Havenga and /or others)?

We talked to everybody who was around at the time, and nobody remembered much about it.

Were there any blueprints or specs of the Moderne ever?

Not that I ever saw. Again, there was a big drawing purge in the early 1970's. When we decided to build a Moderne, we had a friend who had access to an architectural Xerox machine. We provided the nut-to-12th-fret distance of a Gibson scale length and the width of the humbucking pickup, and he scaled the patent drawing up from there. The original peghead would have been over 7" wide, and that wasn't remotely practical, so we reduced its size a bit. It was still pretty huge.

Do you know how many prototypes of the Heritage Modernes there were? (From my research, I found three batches...first 6 with the long stamped serial numbers, and second batch of unknown quantity (my guess is 6) with long stamped serial numbers, and a third batch of 22 with the letter style inked serial numbers.) What was the policy on prototype distribution- did dealers or sales or employees or management get them? To your knowledge, did Gibson ever destroy those types of guitars?

I don't remember how many prototypes there were. It was typical for Gibson to move in several stages to develop guitars at that point in time:

Most prototypes came from R&D, and we'd make them with minimal tooling. They'd be run through the regular production paint and buffing departments, and we'd assemble them. This might have been your first group of six.

After that, the pattern shop would create appropriate tooling and do a pilot run, with a lot more production involvement. If the guitars were to be made in Kalamazoo, that tooling was the basis for the production tooling. (This might be the second group.) If it was a Nashville model, there was a transfer of the appropriate information, and then there would be a Nashville pilot run as well before production began. (This could have been group 3.)

The prototypes would usually go to the appropriate Marketing, management, and production folks. There was no set policy about these, and I don't know if any of the prototypes or pilot run guitars were destroyed.

Is it unheard of to have built "one off" guitars-i.e. a Moderne with a Les Paul neck or a split V headstock? I came across a Moderne with a LP headstock, bound neck,and other out of the ordinary appointments and a serial number that pre dates the earliest prototypes. Personally, I think it was made from parts but I'm not totally sure you guys didn't experiment like that. Present Gibson customer service told me that was never done.

I think this is a parts guitar with a 3-piece neck from another model (probably a flat-topped Les Paul like a Special) and a leftover production Moderne body. I know we never prototyped this incarnation in Kalamazoo. It's got a first-fret position dot, which we wouldn't have done because it wasn't period-correct, and I never would have had a reason to write anything on the bottoms of the pickups, either. (Since I usually assembled the prototypes, I would have been the one to do that.) The serial number appears to have a "501" at the end, and that would have been a Nashville serial number, since the Kalamazoo ones had 0-4 in that slot.

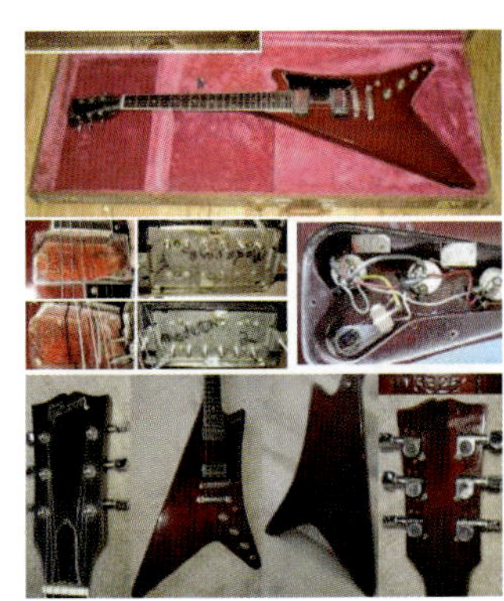

When doing the prototypes, what were you looking for or experimenting with? Was anything changed for production and if so what?

Since we couldn't find an original, we made educated guesses about how it would have been built. It's hard to assemble an original Flying V for several reasons: you have to turn the guitar over several times, you've got a pickguard with controls on it with a separate jack plate, etc. By contrast, the Explorer is much more production-friendly. We designed the modern Moderne the same way. I don't remember what was changed between the first versions and the production ones.

Was there any particular reason for the rectangle case instead of a tapered one?

It was the same outer shape or shell as the Explorer, as I recall, so all that happened was that the inner padding was changed. There was no reason to make a weird fitted shape.

Who made the cases?

I don't remember.

Were the first 6 Heritage Moderne prototypes all done in Mahogany? At what point did you switch to Korina?

Mahogany was both available and cheap; there was no reason to use Korina for the first ones. They probably went to Korina when production began.

Was any other species of wood used besides Mahogany or Korina?

I don't remember any other woods; there would have been no reason to do so.

Were there any records of how many Moderne models were produced?

The record-keeping process gets messy at the end of the Norlin era, and if there were records they would have been at Norlin in Lincolnwood, Ill. After it was sold to Henry and his partners, I remember it was virtually impossible to get shipping records from Norlin.

Is it true that the serial numbers didn't run in sequence- like, B-XXX could have been made one day and F XXX the next?

No. That sequence ran A-xxx, then B-xxx, etc. I think each group's got 100 guitars in it. If a particular guitar had to be refinished or repaired, it would have shipped out of sequence, but they were basically numbered in an ascending sequence.

Who researched the Moderne and what was available from archives?

Mostly, me. Again, there were no archives. There was nothing available.

Were there three runs of prototypes...two with the long stamped serial numbers and a batch with the A-H inked type serials?

Please see the note above. I don't remember exactly what happened with the Moderne.

Was it normal to do two or three runs of prototypes? Why so many?

Please see above.

How would you rate the sales of the Heritage Modernes?

They weren't great; it's a pretty odd guitar.

In your opinion based on your years of experience and research, do you think there were ever any Modernes made in the late 50's or early 60's? (A former Kalamazoo employee told me he saw Modernes there at the Kalamazoo factory in 1963, however Jim Deurloo said he never saw any Modernes, only Explorers.)

For a while, Rem Wall's son Rendall worked in R&D; he's now (I think) at Heritage. He told me in the early 80's that he thinks he might have played a black one in the 1963 Parchment High School production of "Bye Bye Birdie." That's it. If there were more than a very few, I think more people would have remembered them. My best guess is that there may have been a couple, which would have been made by the pattern makers and finished out in the plant.

Which NAMM was the Moderne debuted at? was it Mahogany or Korina, natural or colored?

I don't remember which NAMM and which color; sorry.

Before Henry took over Gibson and stopped doing "seconds", what determined if a guitar was cut up or saved?

A minor cosmetic flaw made the guitar a #2, and these were sold to dealers. A major cosmetic flaw, or a structural issue that left the guitar still playable would make it a bargain, (BGN) and those were sold to employees once or twice a year. If it was seriously screwed up, they might save the neck or the body and recycle them into production or repair.

Could employees build stuff on their own time?

No.

Was there some kind of employee purchase plan in effect?

Yes, employees could buy guitars.

Why did Gibson want to close the Kalamazoo plant?

This is a long story, and I don't have all the information, but basically they felt they only needed one facility and there was no reason to keep the old one when they had a nice new one.

Was there some kind of an auction when the Kalamazoo plant closed? I know lots of people who somehow got parts,bodies,necks and so forth. I was wondering how they were able to obtain that stuff.

I don't remember how this worked, but it's obvious a lot of stuff got, shall we say, dispersed.

Ever heard of Frank D'Angelo or Reno Alberti?

Nope.

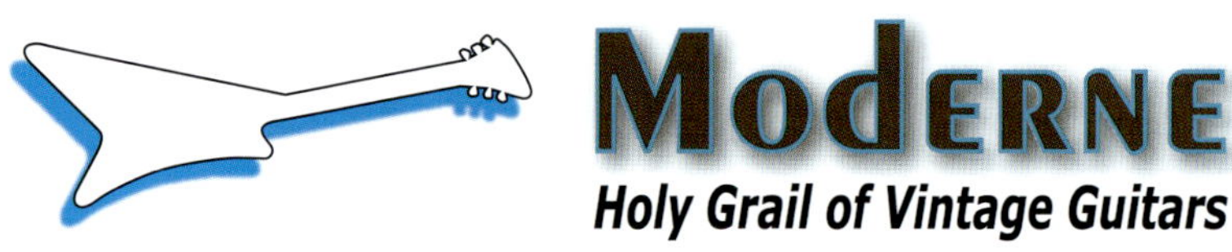

Billy Gibbons has what he thinks is an original Moderne and he said that he brought it to Gibson(I don't know if it was Kalamazoo or Nashville) to have it checked out...did you ever get to see it?(photo below for ya. It's the best photo I have of it. So far Billy has not gotten back to me about it)

I mean no disrespect to Mr. Gibbons and I've never examined this guitar, but my gut instinct would be that it's another parts guitar, with a Gibson neck and a body made off the patent drawing. The pickguard shape is visually not consistent with Gibson pickguards of the period; even though we've never seen one we know to be correct, it just doesn't look "right."

The truss rod cover on the Moderne...why was it different?

We thought the bell truss rod cover looked weird on the "Gumby" peghead, and there was no truss rod cover shown on the patent drawing. Chuck Burge came up with that one.

Why the special serial numbers A-H?

Bruce Bolen felt that the alphanumeric designations conferred more value that a large batch of serial numbers. Instead of "12345678987654" or whatever, you would have B016.

Since sales for the Moderne were so poor, do you know if the wood for the Modernes was sacrificed in favor of Flying V's?

Sacrifice is the wrong term. You have x amount of wood. You have no orders for Modernes, and 150 orders for Flying V's. What do you do?

Who first suggested the idea of making the Moderne to include in the Heritage Series? How did they even know about that particular model?

Again, "they" is "we", which is to say Bruce Bolen and the guys in R&D. We pioneered that model-Marketing didn't suggest it. Unless you've got a catalogue showing it listed in the Heritage Series—and I don't---I don't think it was part of that. It really doesn't matter that much: we were looking for interesting stuff to sell. Marketing figured out the categories to put it in.

About the Billy Gibbons Moderne and the one Dan Erlewine had: both of these guitars were acquired in 1970 and 1971. That predates any of the Ibanez Copies. Almost no one had heard of the Moderne back then. Why would someone make a copy of a guitar that never really was and how would they know about it? I've looked at both the Billy G and the Dan E. Moderne photos many times. They a very similar and both sport the giant pickguard. Probably made by the same person don't you think?

anyway...that's why I asked you about this Reno Alberti guy. I was told that he worked briefly at Gibson somewhere around 57-63. He was let go for some reason and allegedly took some stuff home with him-including the "blueprints" for the Moderne. This guy is reported to be the builder of those two guitars. I haven't been able to verify any of that info but that's what I was told from two different sources. I just think it's very unusual for a Moderne to surface in the early 70's and they are pretty much identical. What do you think?

I don't disagree that this is unusual, but I really don't have an explanation for it, either. Neither Bruce nor I has ever heard or Reno Alberti. Jim Hutchins might know—he started at Gibson in 1958. Dan Erlewine's still around, of course—it would be interesting to get his explanation for how he acquired his "Moderne."

Even in the early '70's there's a certain vintage awareness. Guys like George Gruhn and Matt Umanov were active then, and as a repairman in Kalamazoo I saw a lot of old guitars and was looking at a lot of weird stuff that Gibson had built—models that didn't quite exist that had been sold off to employees when they weren't introduced, etc. It's not unreasonable for folks back then to have been interested in guitars like the Moderne and Futura—these were "holy Grail" Gibsons, like the White Penguin and Marauder were for Gretsch and Fender. A clever fellow could have built one outside the factory. I don't know why, but it would have been possible. It's widely reported that the Explorer, V, and Moderne were all shown at NAMM in 1959, so there should be one original around, anyway. I just don't think those two are "it."

Here's how it might have gone when Gibson built a Moderne, assuming that they really did: Even when I was at Gibson, it was common practice to do a prototype, take it to NAMM, and then build them if they sold. We were capable of building guitars with very little in the way of engineering packages. A Moderne could have been drawn up full-size, they made a 1:1 copy of the body drawing and the peghead, then the pattern shop would have glued the drawing to a blank and band-sawn the body. They would have used existing tooling for the pickup holes and bridge/tailpiece locators. (The Gibbons "Moderne," if it's real, should have some very specific dimensions in the pickup holes and some tell-tale tooling marks. There are particular distances involved in the bridge and tailpiece locations as well. There would have been little reason to have free-handed these items.)

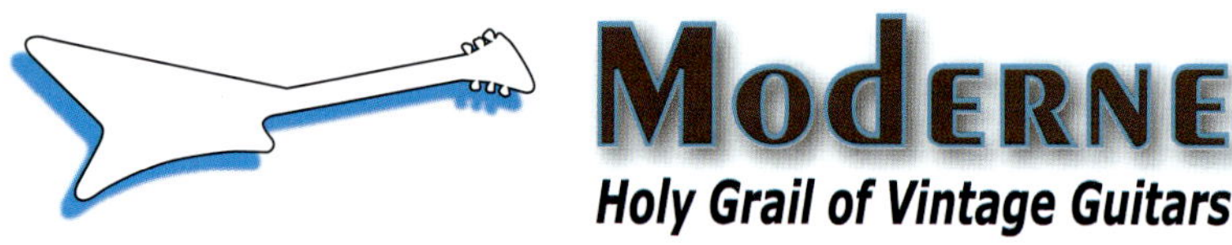

Let's consider the neck: If you didn't shape the peghead out, you could have used the Les Paul Junior templates to make the Moderne neck, since both the Les Paul and the Moderne join at the 16th fret, and they would have had about the same neck angle. It would have been relatively easy to glue on larger "ears" to make the peghead wider, and then to have cut out one "Gumby" peghead on the bandsaw. Again, we did this kind of stuff all the time; it's really not that hard. The Kalamazoo tooling setup made it relatively easy to put "Peghead A" on "Neck B".

I guess I still have a very hard time with the pickguard on the Gibbons/Erlewine guitars because it has nothing whatever to do with the body shape. Many Gibson designs have an almost "Classical" feel to their proportions. Or, for that matter, look at these pickguards:

Les Paul
Flying V
Explorer
Firebird
L-5
J-45
SG
Hummingbird (yeah, it's large and pointy, but all the curves are smooth.)

Now look at that "Moderne" pickguard. By comparison, it looks like a 7-year old did it. It's weird and it's not at all elegant. These other Gibson pickguards were done with French curve sets; this one looks like it was done at arm's length with a crayon. It's really ugly, and it's not stylistically like any other Gibson pickguard I've ever seen. In the end, I can't believe a Gibson Engineer of that day got paid to do it.

Ren Wall - Heritage Guitars

I just did an interview with Tim Shaw and he told me that you told him you might have at one time played a Gibson Moderne in 1963 at Parchment High School... is that true?

This is the type I played in Bye Bye Birdie, many years ago at the Barn Theater in Augusta, MI. I put it back in the old Gibson morgue, up over Julius Bellson's old office.

It was so-ooo ugly, but wish I had it today. Think someone from NORLIN came over and cleaned house years ago, and I never saw it again.

Rumor has it, that someone offered me a million for it if I still had it, and believe me, if I did, it would have been long gone. Probably could have bought it for less than a hundred back then.

Tim Shaw told me he doesn't think Gibson would have made the pickguard like that.

Tim is right. It had a different finger rest.

I was told Stan Rendell had a Moderne hanging on his wall...wonder if your guitar was it?

Don't remember Stan having one on the wall. I never owned one, just played it in "BYE BYE BIRDIE" Sorry, wish I had more info.

Chapter 10
Photos

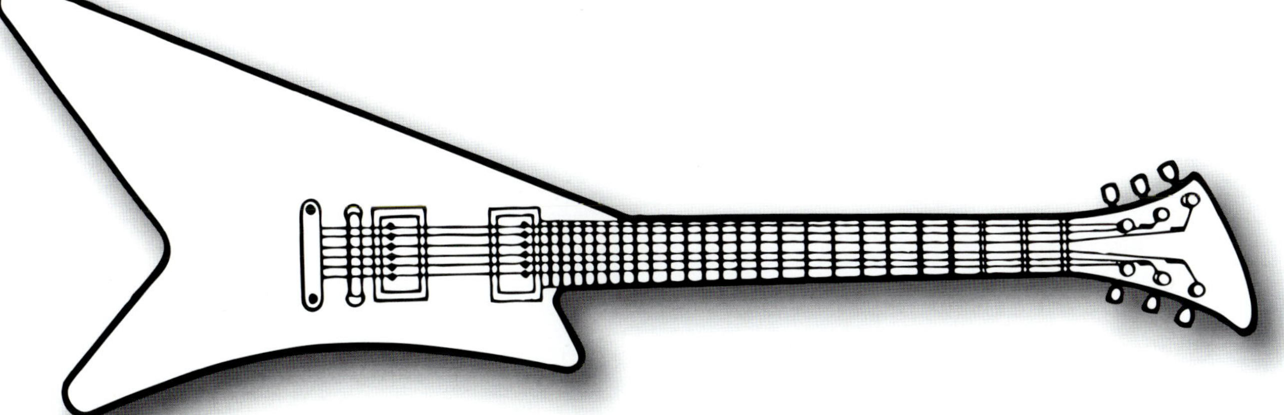

Moderne
Holy Grail of Vintage Guitars

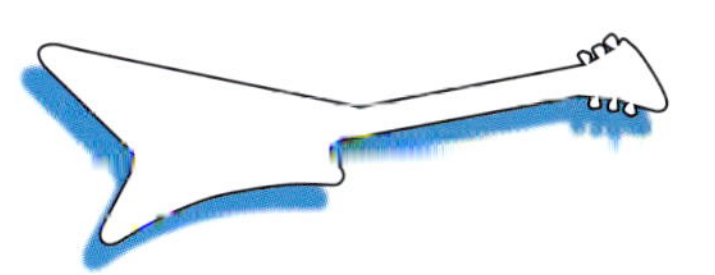

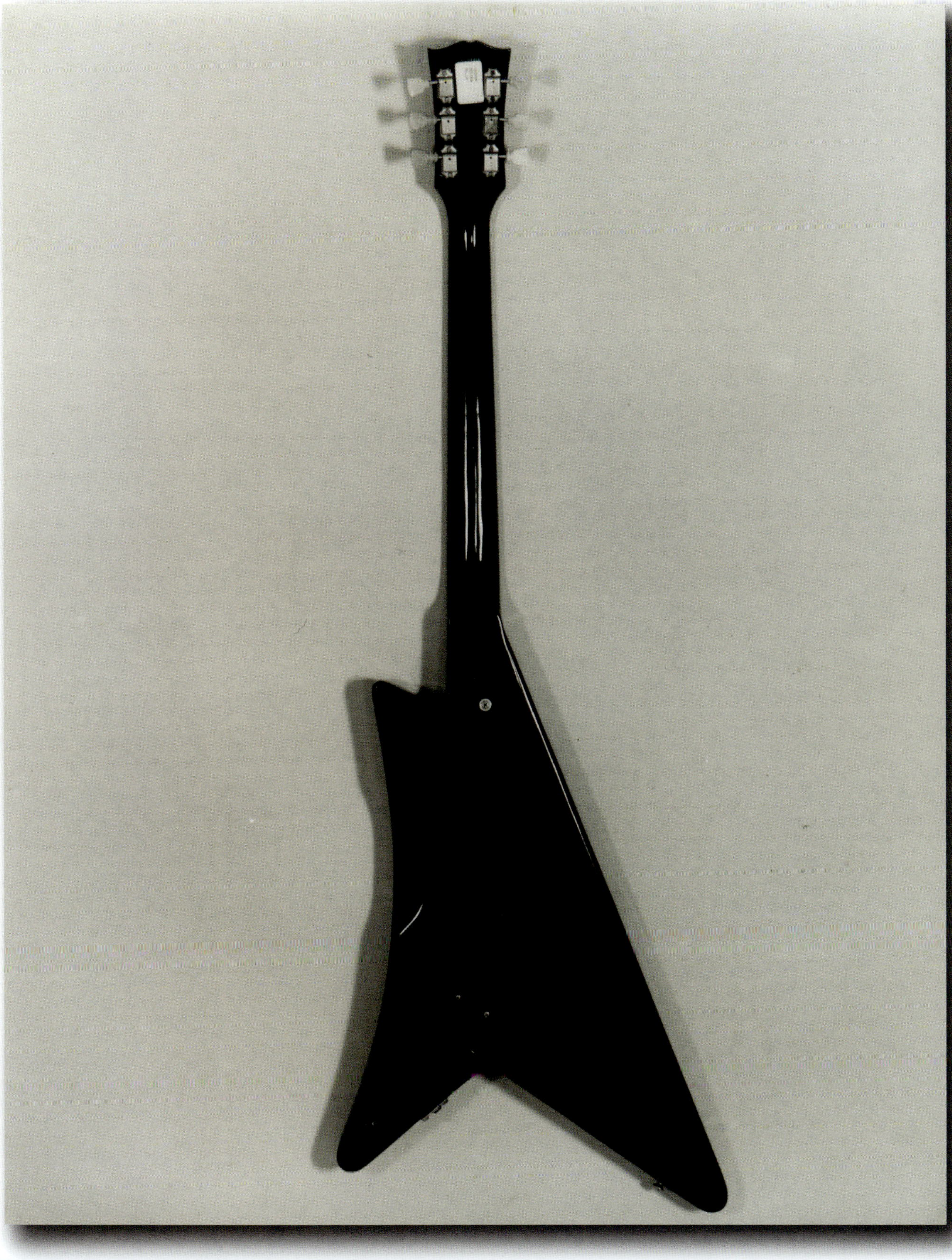

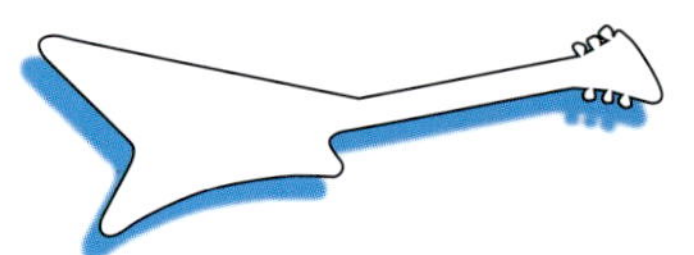

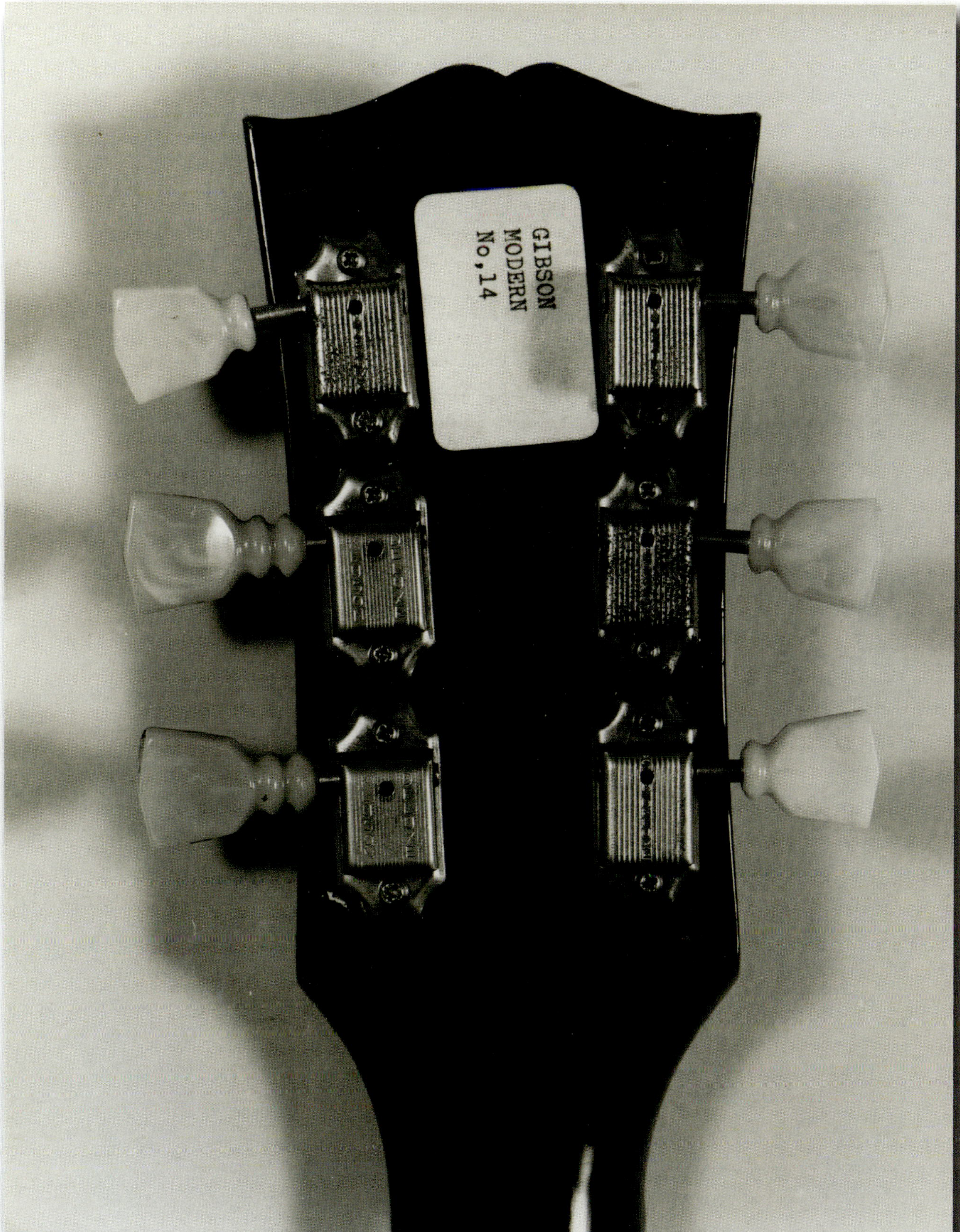

Gibson Moderne Serial # A 057

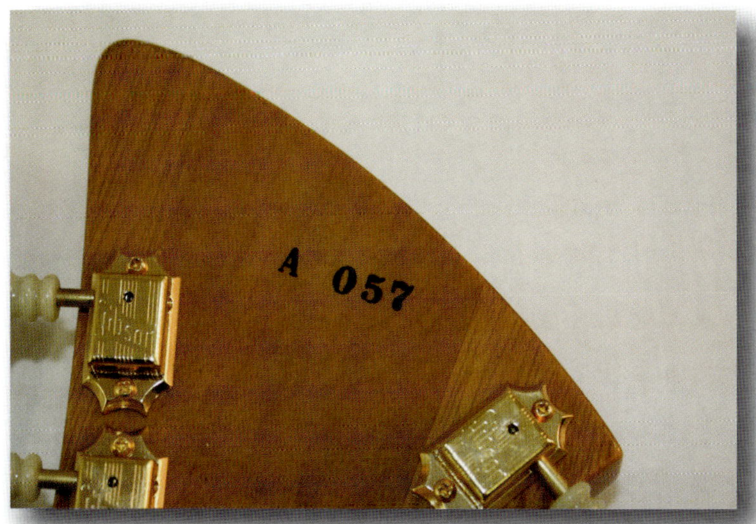

Photos©Dave's Guitar

Gibson Moderne Serial # A 072

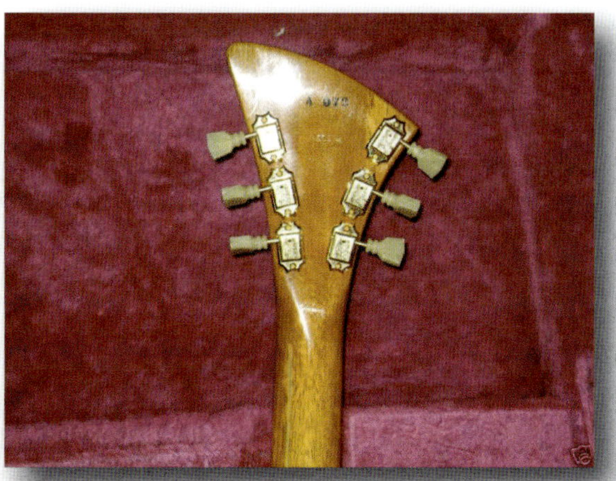

Gibson Moderne Serial # B 028

Serial # -Has been removed
it was B 028
Pots date to 1980 and 1981.

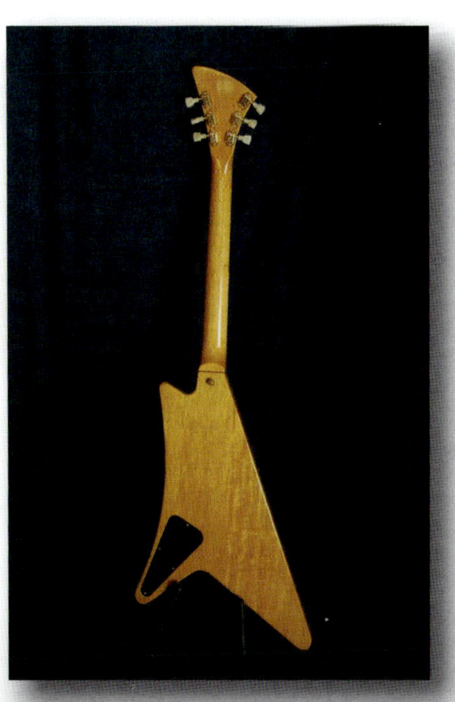

Gibson Moderne
Serial # C 001

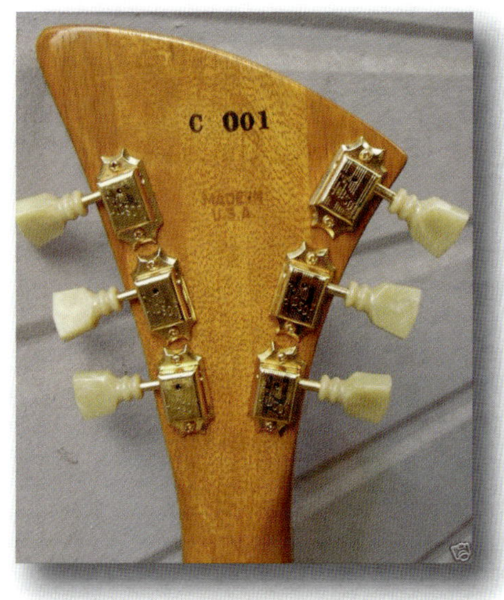

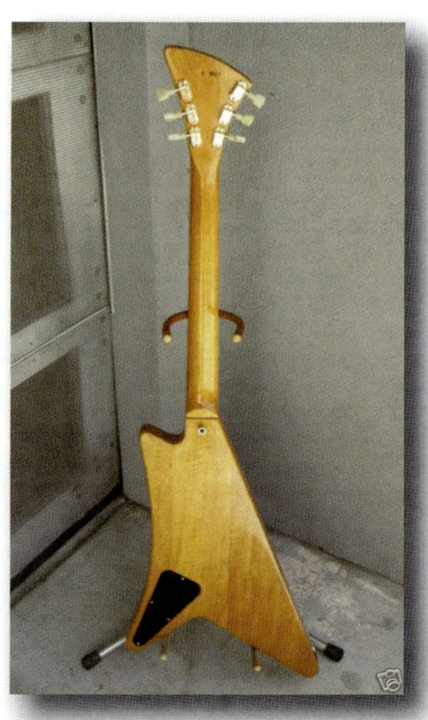

Gibson Moderne Serial # C 089

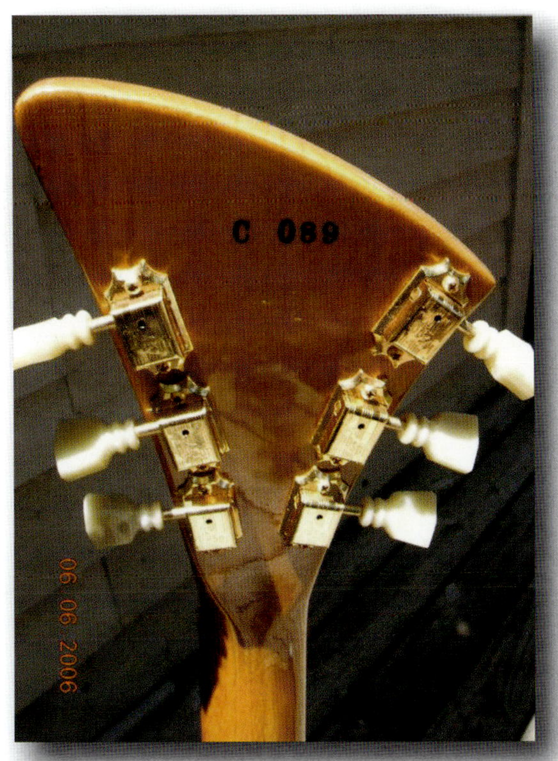

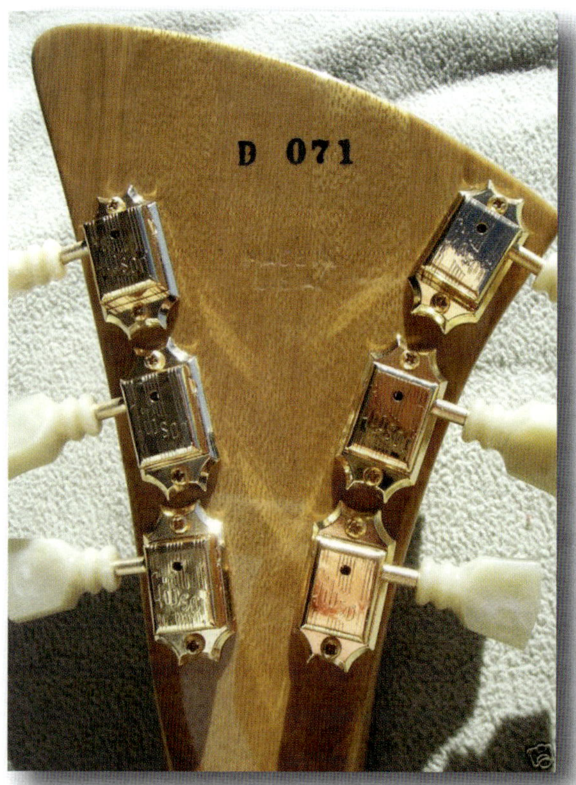

Gibson Moderne Serial # D 071

Gibson Moderne
Serial # E 099

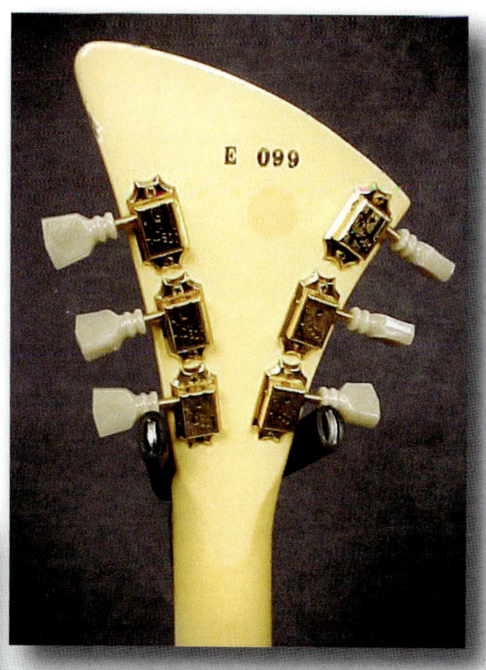

Photos©Elderly Instruments

Gibson Moderne
Serial # F 020

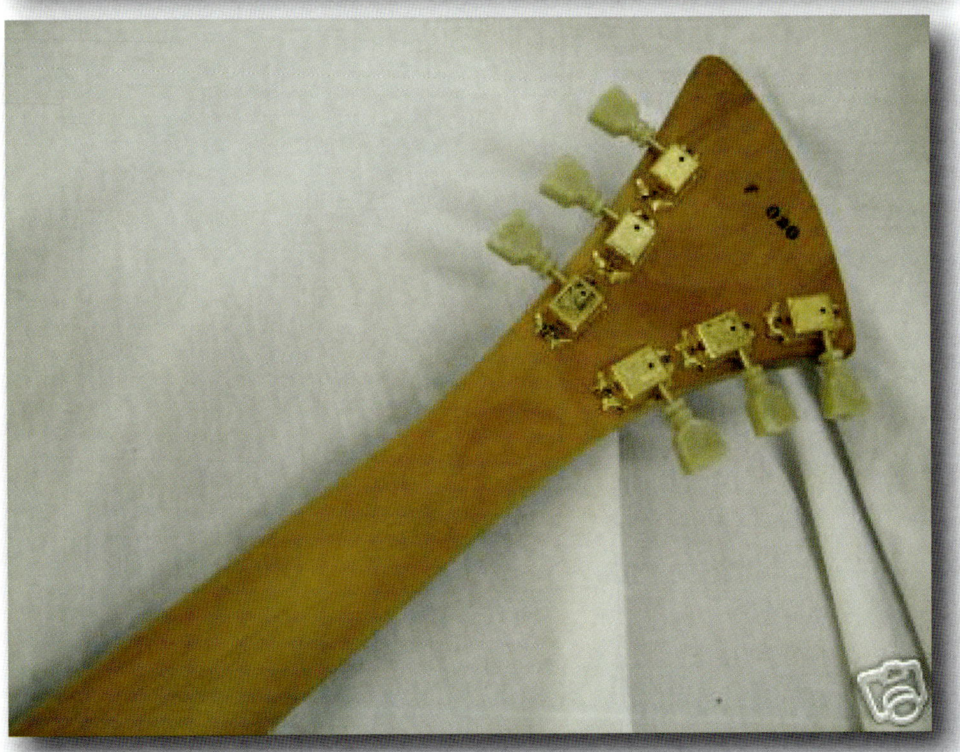

Gibson Moderne
Serial # G 026

Gibson Moderne
Serial # G 060

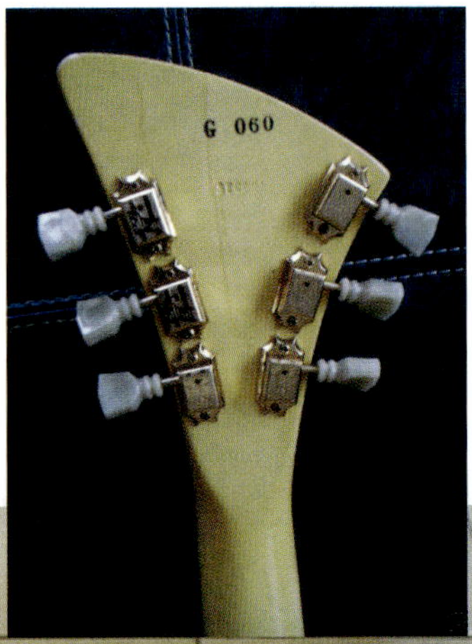

Gibson Moderne
Serial # G 089

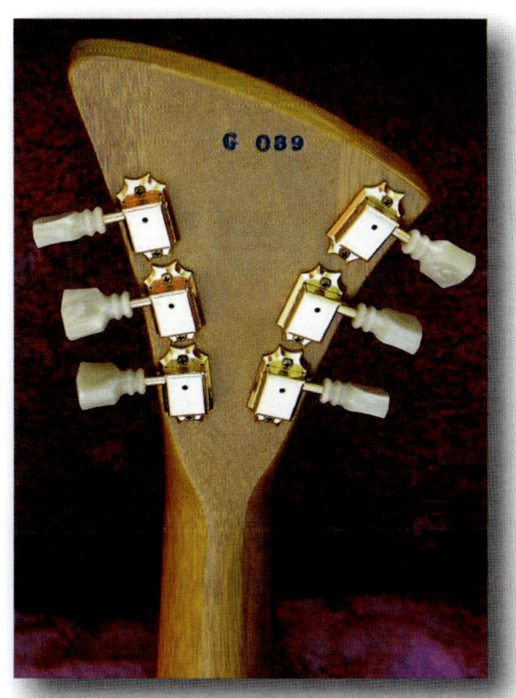

Gibson Moderne
Serial # H 014

Gibson Moderne
Serial # H 027

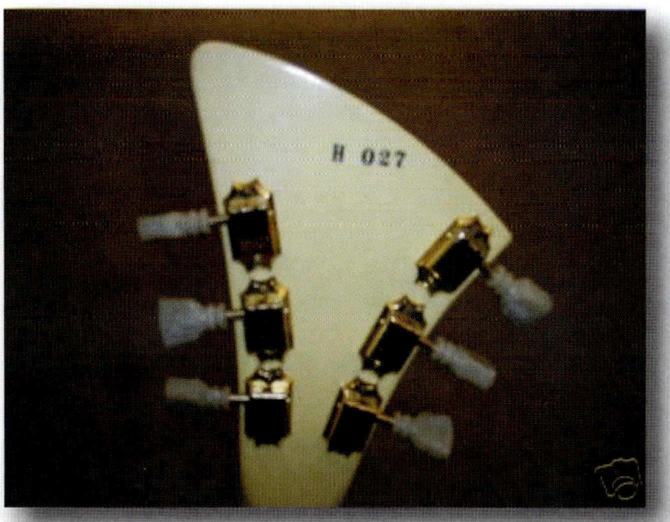

Gibson Moderne
Serial # H 037

Wrona's House Of Violins

Glen Miller has many years of experience in instrument repair, building, finishing, customizing and replicas. Glen also has experience in guitar manufacturing from the raw wood to a finished product.

Wrona's was fortunate to have obtained a supply of old stock Kalamazoo made Gibson parts, from a former Gibson employee, some of which are shown below.

Because of unprecedented access to authentic vintage Gibson parts, Wrona's are now offering custom made recreations of vintage Gibson style guitars. They re-create these vintage models such as 1955 through 1961 Les Paul Specials and Juniors. They also offer very accurate Explorers, Flying V's, and Moderne's with the very rare split V headstock.

Glenn Miller built this Moderne from Gibson parts leftover from the Kalamazoo Factory.Serial # 8 2377

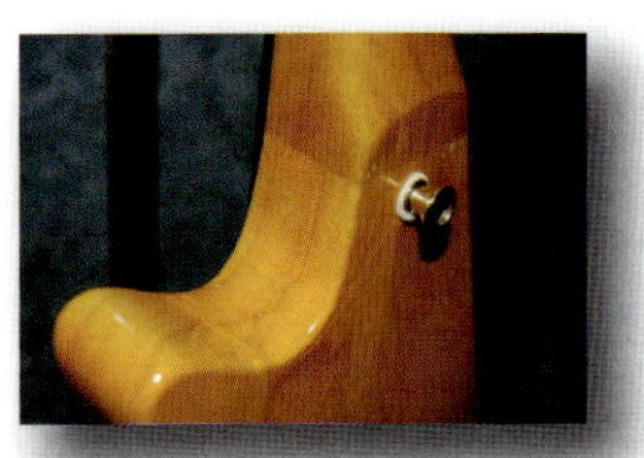

Gibson
Gibson
Gibson

I was curious how Glenn was able to get all these Gibson parts and bodies so I gave him a call. He did in fact get the parts from an ex Gibson employee who didn't want his name revealed. Glenn told me he could build me a custom Moderne with all the "correct routes" and a "real Gibson neck" and leave it unfinished and without parts for around $800 to $1100. He sold the split headstock Mahogany Moderne for $4000 and the korina Moderne for $3500.

Two of Glenn Miller's completed Moderne guitars. Mahogany on the left, Korina on the right.

1983 Mahogany Moderne. Obtained from an ex Gibson employee. who had a supply of parts and hardware he obtained when Gibson moved out of Kalamazoo in early 1984. This may be the only Moderne with Futura headstock.

Photos©Wayne Joseph

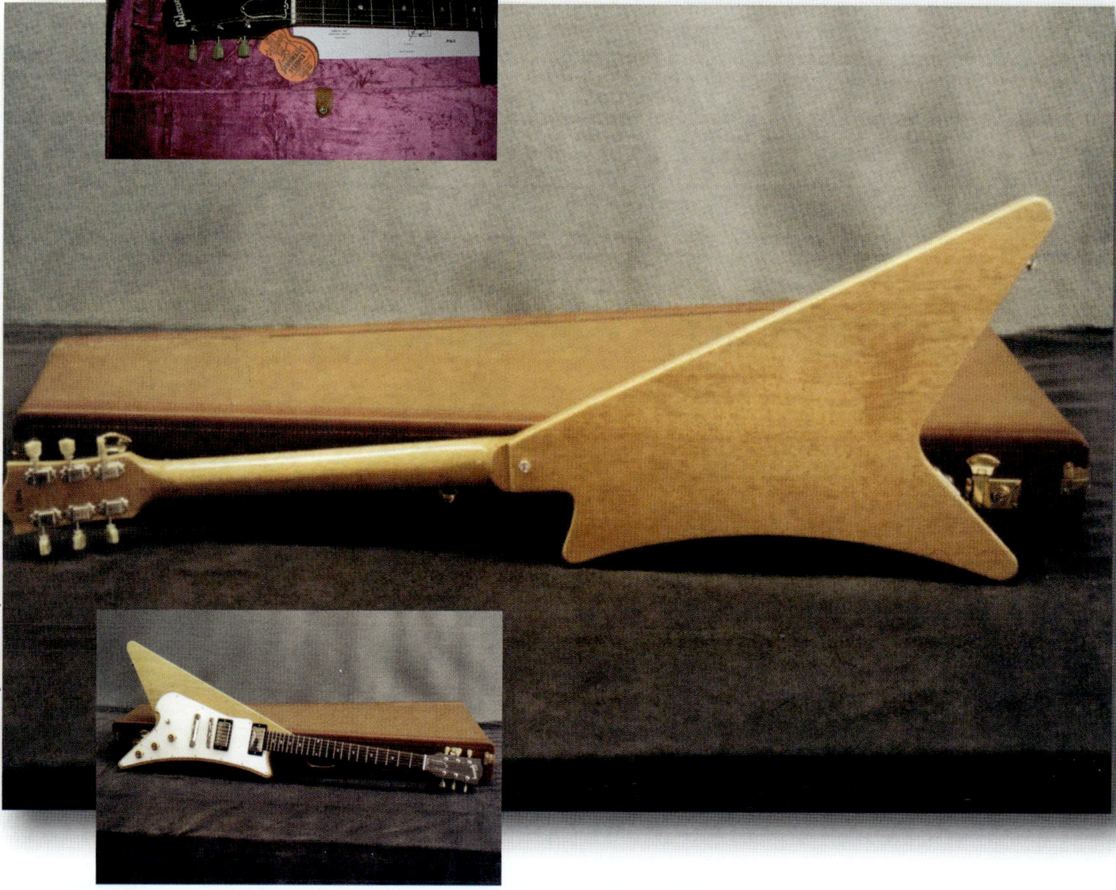

Photos©Wayne Joseph

The Components of the Moderne Electric Guitar

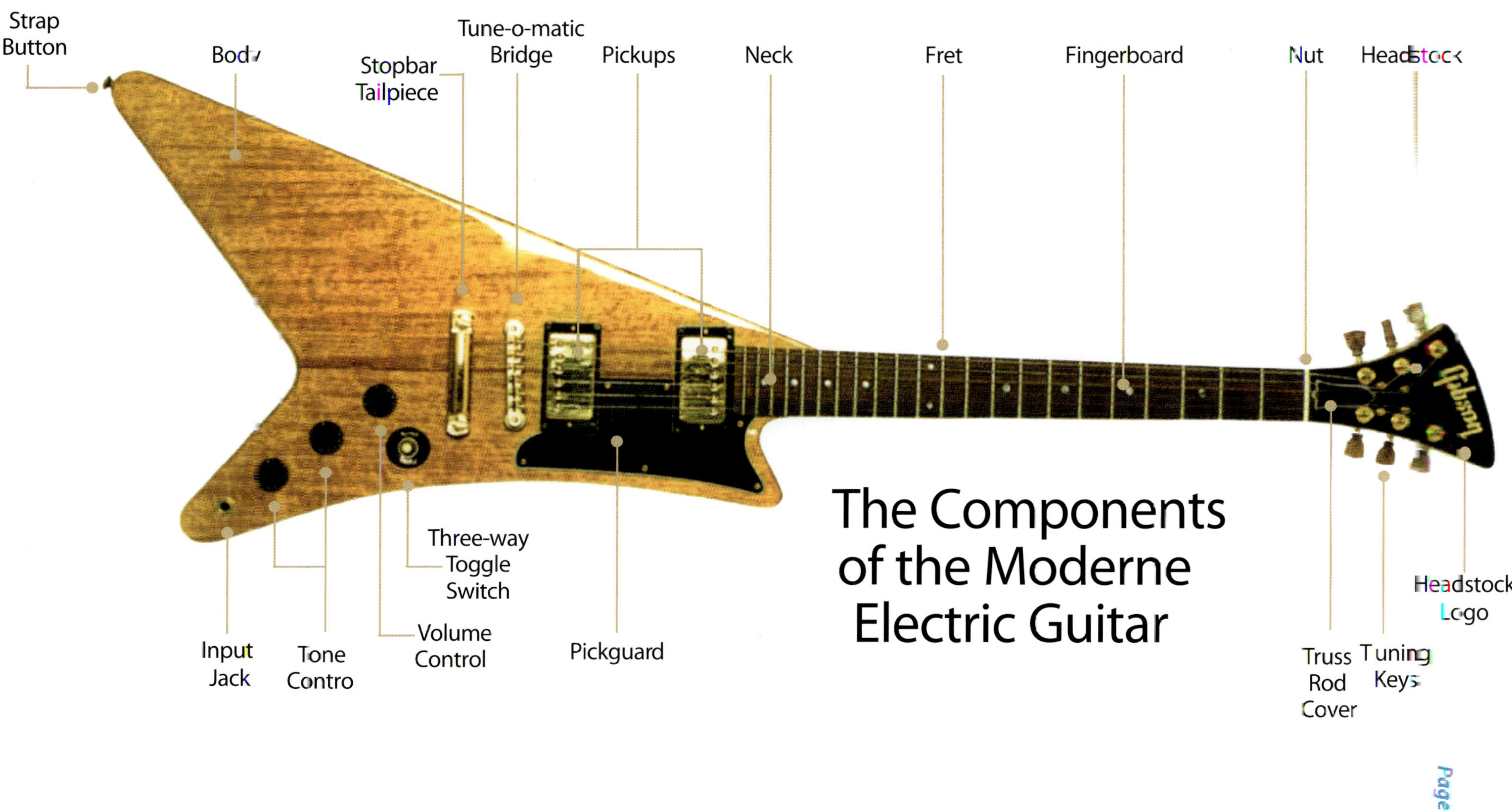

Serial Numbers

Below is a partial list of serial numbers I've compiled of Gibson Moderne guitars that were verified with photos. If you wish to add to the list, please send me an email.

82262015 (Prototype) Red
82282013 (Prototype) Ebony
82282014 (Prototype) Ebony
82282016 (Prototype) Natural Mahogany
82282017 (Prototype) Red
82282023 (Prototype) Black

A 001 (Prototype) Red
A 002 (Prototype) Natural Korina
A 003 (Prototype) Natural Korina
A 009 (Prototype) Natural Korina
A 044 Natural Korina
A 046 Natural Korina
A 057 Natural Korina
A 072 Natural Korina
A 084 Natural Korina

B 028 Natural Korina (Serial # was removed)
B 030 Black
B 036 Natural Korina
B 052 Natural Korina
B 067 Natural Korina (Factory Kahler Tremolo)
B 082 Natural Korina

C 001 Natural Korina
C 033 Natural Korina
C 086 Natural Korina
C 089 Natural Korina

D 009 Natural Korina
D 051 Natural Korina
D 054 Natural Korina
D 071 Natural Korina
D 095 Natural Korina
D 100 Natural Korina

E 040 Black (Factory Kahler Tremolo)
E 099 White

F 020 Natural Korina
F 036 Natural Korina
F 039 White
F 077 Natural Korina
F 094 Natural Korina
F 097 Natural Korina

G 025 Natural Korina
G 026 Natural Korina
G 056 White
G 060 White
G 073 Natural Korina
G 089 Natural Korina

H 014 White
H 027 White
H 036 Natural Korina
H 037 Black
H 049 White
H 073 White

Appendix

• A Heritage Moderne existed with serial number 8 3922. 

• At least two Modernes built by Glenn Miller have serial numbers in the 8 XXXX format.

• Supposedly there is a Moderne and matching Explorer in Bahama Blue.
• Supposedly there is a tobacco sunburst prototype of the Heritage Moderne.
• A former kalamazoo Gibson employee told me he saw completed Modernes at the factory in 1963. He would not go on record with that information.
• Ed Campbell said he doesn't know either Alberti Reno or George Manno.
• There might have been a left handed Heritage Moderne made.
• Some Heritage Modernes came equipped with factory installed Kahler tremolos.
• Blue Book of Electric Guitars says the reissue Moderne specs were taken from the blueprint. Walter Carter told me he thinks they mean the patent drawing. He said there is no blueprint.
• Gary at Guitars West claims he knows someone who has what they claim is an original Moderne. He has seen no evidence of it yet.
• Ren at Heritage Guitars informed me that the man in this photo is Howard Quibell and he has passed away.
• I asked Ted McCarty's daughter about Frank D'Angelo ..She never heard of Frank D'Angelo. D'Angelo is the guy who supposedly built 2 of the original modernes and was supposed to be good friends with Ted.
• I asked Ren at Heritage Guitars about Frank D'Angelo, none of the guys who worked at Gibson in 1956 till the plant in Kalamazoo closed ever heard of Frank D'Angelo.

Source Materials

Books:

- American Guitars - Tom Wheeler ISBN 0-06-014996-5, pgs 143,172,173,176
- The Gibson Electric Guitar Book - Walter Carter ISBN 0-87930-895-8 pgs 52, 53, 54, 55
- Gibson Guitars 100 Years of an American Icon - Walter Carter ISBN 0972751017 pgs 210-215
- Bass Culture - The John Entwistle Bass Collection ISBN 1-86074-593-8 pg 186-187
- Gibson Electrics - A.R. Duchossoir ISBN 0-88188-269-0 pgs 91-99, 179
- Gibson Electrics - The Classic Years -A.R. Duchossoir ISBN 0-7935-3124-1 pgs 69-75
- The Electric Guitar - Nick Freeth & Charles Alexander ISBN 0-7624-0522-8 pgs 84,85
- The Gibson ISBN 1-85909-302-7 pgs 29,47,54,134,135,156
- Guitar Trader's Vintage Guitar Bulletin Vol 1 ISBN 0-933224-58-3
  October 1982 Vol 1 No. 6 pg 22
  December 1982 Vol 1 No. 8 pg 1
- Blue Book Of Electric Guitars 9th Edition - Zachary R. Fjested ISBN 1-886768-57-9 pg 421
- ZZ Top Bad And Worldwide - Deborah Frost ISBN 0-02-002950-0 pg. 80
- The Gibson Story - Julius Bellson ASIN: B0006CBFJC

Magazines:

- Vintage Guitar Magazine,September 1993 Page 38 Moderne: Fact or fiction By Cohn Rude
- Vintage Guitar Magazine, April 1999 Ted McCarty,I'm Not a Musician By Willie G. Moseley
- Guitar Player,
- Piano Trade,

Internet web sites:

- www.ebay.com
- www.gibson.com
- www.universalmetropolis.com/city/threads.php?threadid=14435
- http://guitarplayer.com/article/will-rays-ebay/Jan-04/936
- http://www.u-magazine.com/magazine/articles.php?articleid=1142
- www.namm.org
- http://www.cigaraficionado.com/Cigar/CA_Features/CA_Feature_Basic_Template/0,2344,599,00.html
- http://www.allduff.com/sights_gibsonmoderne.htm
- http://www.intersilo.com/gibson.asp
- http://www.gibson.com/products/gibson/Stories/Designer.html
- http://www.ibanezcollectors.com/

Interviews:

- Phone interview with Cohn Rude 2007
- Phone interview with Watler Carter 2007
- Phone interview with George Gruhn 2007
- Phone interview with Dan Erlewine 2007
- Phone interview with Geroge Manno 2007
- Phone interview with Bill Antel 2007
- Phone interview with Scott Matteson 2007
- Phone interview with Dennis Chandler 2008
- Phone interview with Glenn Miller 2008
- Phone interview with Michael Stevens 2007
- Phone interview with Howard Leese 2008
- Phone interview with Tom Bradfield 2008
- Phone interview with Wayne Joeseph 2008

Email:

- email correspondence with Walter Carter • Chris Grimmett • Frank Lucido • Peter Fung • Rondy Burgett • Tony Arambarri • Zachary Fjestad
- Erick Coleman • Wayne Joeseph •

Suggested Reading

Guitar Related

Gibson Guitars: Ted McCarty's Golden Era: 1948-1966: Gil Hembree
The Early Years Of The Les Paul Legacy 1915-1963: Robb Lawrence
The Acoustic Guitar Voulme 2: Don E. Teeter
The Beauty of the 'Burst: Yasuhiko Iwanad
'Burst 1958-'60 Sunburst Les Paul: Jay Scott & Vic Da Pra
50 Years of the Gibson Les Paul: Tony Bacon
Gibson Elecrics: A.R.Duchossoir
Gibson Electrics, The Classic Years: A.R.Duchossoir
Gibson Guitars, 100 Years of an American Icon: Walter Carter
The Gibson Les Paul Book: Tony Bacon
The Gibson Guitar from 1950 Vol 1&2: Ian C. Bishop
Flying V, The Illustrated History of this Modernistic Guitar: Larry Meiners
Classic Guitars of the 50's: various authors
Guitar Player Repair Guide: Dan Erlewine
Gruhn's Guide to Vintage Guitars: George Gruhn
Guitar Identification: Andre Duchossoir
The Complete Guitarist: Richard Chapman
Classic Guitar Making: Authur E. Overholtzer
Guitar Electronics, a workbook: Donald Brosnac
Electronic Projects for Musicians: Craig Anderton
Complete Guitar Repair: Hideo Kamimoto
The Steel String Guitar, it's History and Construction: Donald Brosnac
Electric Guitar Construction: Tom Hirst
The Illustrated History of the Electric Guitar: Michael Heatly
The Guitar: Terrance Ashley
The Ultimate Guitar Book: Tony Bacon
Constructing a Solid Body Guitar: Roger Siminoff
Make Your Own Electric Guitar: Melvyn Hiscock
Vintage Guitar: The Bold Strummer(reprinted Guitar Trader articles)
Trade Secrets Volumes 1&2: Stew-Mac Shopguide Series
An introduction to Scientific Guitar Design: Donald Brosnac
Fret Work Step by Step: Dan Erlewine (Stew-Mac Shopguide Series)
Make Your Own Spanish Guitar: A.P.Sharpe
Classic Guitar Maker's Guide: H.E. Brown
Electric Guitar Maker's Guide: H.E. Brown
The Electric Guitar: A History of an American Icon
The Story of the Fender Stratocaster: Ray Minhinnett & Bob Young

Amp Related

The Amp Book: Donald Brosnac
Inside Tube Amps: Dan Torres
The Tube Amp Book: Aspen Pittman
The Complete Guide to Guitar and Amp Maintenence: Ritchie Flieger
How to service your own tube amp: Tom Mitchell
Building vacuum tube guitar and bass amplifiers vol 1&2: Tino Zottola
Reference Data for Radio Engineers: IT&T Corporation
Basic Vacuum Tubes and their uses: John F. Rider and Henry Jacobowitz
How to repair musical instrument amplifiers: Byron Wels
RCA Receiving Tube Manual: RCA Corporation
Fender Amps, the first 50 years: Teagle & Sprung
The Professional Audio SourceBook Volume 2: B&H

About the author:

Ronald has been a musician for 29 years, has studied all facets of guitar building, repair, and design and worked in the Gibson Custom Shop in Memphis . He currently resides in Gainesville, Florida.

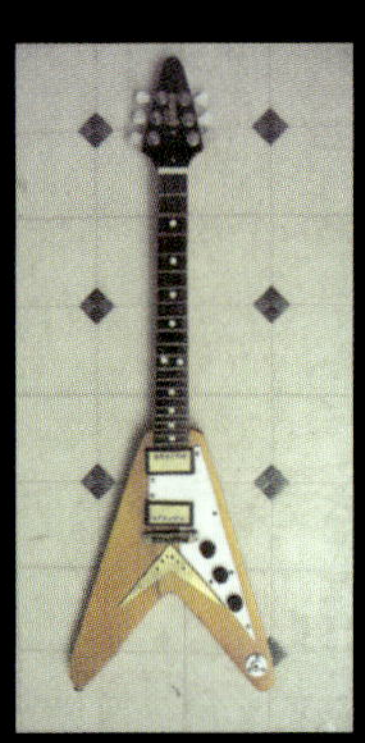

For questions, suggestions, or comments, or if you have pictures or information to share, please email

More Great Books from Centerstream...

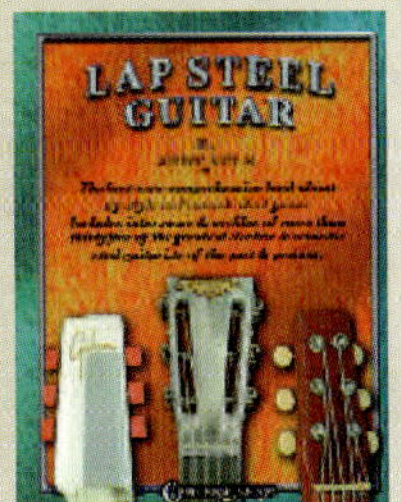

LAP STEEL GUITAR

by Andy Volk

This first ever comprehensive book about lap-steel and console steel guitars includes: interviews and profiles of more than 35 of the greatest electric and acoustic steel guitarists of the past and present, representing most forms of music played in the world today. Also includes resources for guitars, amplifiers, accessories, instructional materials, steel guitar tunings; and much more.

00000320 336 pages $35.00

THE LARSONS' CREATIONS – CENTENNIAL EDITION

Guitars & Mandolins

by Robert Carl Hartman

This book is an account of two brothers who were premier producers of stringed instruments in the early part of this century. Swedish immigrant cabinet makers Carl and August Larson made instruments under the brand names of Maurer, Prairie State, Euphonon, W.J. Dyer & Bro., Wm. C. Stahl, and under their own name, and their highly collectible creations are considered today to be some of the finest ever made. This volume includes 16 pages of full-color photos, classic advertisements and catalogs, and a CD featuring guitarist Muriel Anderson playing 11 songs on 11 Larson instruments.

00001043 Hardcover Book/CD Pack $65.00
00001042 Softcover Book/CD Pack $45.00

MAKING AN ARCHTOP GUITAR

by Robert Benedetto

The definitive work on the design and construction of an acoustic archtop guitar by one of the most talented luthiers of the twentieth century. Benedetto shows all aspects of construction, even through marketing your finished work. Includes a list of suppliers; a list of serial numbers for Benedetto guitars; full-color plates; photos from the author's personal scrapbook; and fold-out templates.

00000174 260 pages $39.95

MUSIC MAN: 1978 TO 1982 (AND THEN SOME!)

The Other Side of the Story

by Frank W/M Green

Legendary for their construction and longevity, Music Man amps have earned the trust and respect of musicians worldwide. The company was the brainchild of industry vets Leo Fender, Forrest White, and Tom Walker. This book examines the latter – the company's "genius chief pilot/navigator" – particularly during the productive epoch from 1978 to 1982.

00001100 .... $24.95

PICKUPS, WINDINGS AND MAGNETS

... And the Guitar Became Electric

by Mario Milan

Guitar collectors rejoice! The first book to examine pickups in detail is here! Covers everything from the first experiments to classic models conceived for Rickenbacker, Gibson, Fender, Gretsch, Danelectro, Epiphone, and others, with an overview of Japanese and European manufacturers. Includes a 32-page color section of the most popular models and rarities, a timeline, info on building pickups and technical specs, and biographical notes on George Beauchamp, Leo Fender, Seth Lover, Larry DiMarzio, and Seymour Duncan.

00001026 .... $29.95

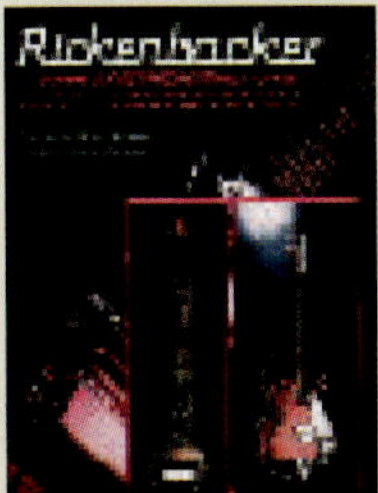

RICKENBACKER

by Richard Smith

A complete and illustrated history of the development of Rickenbacker instruments from 1931 to the present, complete with information and full-color photos of the many Rickenbacker artists.

00000098 256 pages $35.00

WASHBURN PREWAR INSTRUMENT STYLES

Guitars, Mandolins, Banjos and Ukuleles 1883-1940

By Hubert Pleijsier

The vintage guitar collecting market continues to grow. This book is the first of its kind to report on pre-war Washburn guitars, mandolins, banjos and ukuleles. It contains detailed information about more than 450 instrument styles, serial numbering schemes and estimated production totals. A gorgeous 32-page color photo section of the most collectibles will make this book a "must" for players and collectors alike.

00001176 272 pages $45.00

RING THE BANJAR!

The Banjo in America from Folklore to Factory

by Robert Lloyd Webb

This is a second edition of a publication originally published to coincide with an exhibition of the same name at the Massachusetts Institute of Technology Museum. Includes information on the banjo's enduring popularity, the banjo makers of Boston, instruments from the exhibition, a glossary and bibliography of the banjo, and more.

00000087 102 pages $24.95

P.O. Box 17878 - Anaheim Hills, CA 92817
(714) 779-9390 www.centerstream-usa.com

More Great Books from Centerstream...

COWBOY GUITARS

by Steve Evans and Ron Middlebrook
foreword by Roy Rogers, Jr.

Back in the good old days, all of America was infatuated with the singing cowboys of movies and radio. This huge interest led to the production of "cowboy guitars." This fun, fact-filled book is an outstanding roundup of these wonderful instruments.

00000281 Softcover (232 pages)........................$35.00
00000303 Hardcover (234 pages)........................$55.00

THE GIBSON 'BURST
1958-1960

by Jay Scott and Vic DaPra
forewords by Jimmy Page and Robby Krieger

A musical instrument or a cultural icon? Certainly, the Gibson Les Paul "Sunburst" Standard has become the single most desirable and collectable electric guitar ever made. The late '50s middle-of-the-road guitar emerges as the turn-of-the-century Holy Grail. With over 300 'Bursts shown and 16 pages of full color photos, this is the book for all collectors. Also includes a 1958, '59, and '60 Sunburst Les Paul serial number list.

"Since the first publication of this book 'til today, the Sunburst has continued to inspire me and new generations of musicians. Thank you, Les."
– Jimmy Page

00000423 Softcover........................$35.00
00000477 Hardcover........................$50.00

THE GIBSON 175
Its History and Its Players

by Adrian Ingram

Debuting in 1949 and in continuous production ever since, the ES-175 is one of the most versatile and famous guitars in music history. The first Gibson electric to feature a Florentine cutaway, the ES-175 was also one of the first Electric Spanish guitars to be fitted with P.A.F. humbuckers and is prized for its playability, craftsmanship, and full rich tone. Written by noted author/guitarist Adrian Ingram, contents include: the complete history of the 175, The Players, a beautiful ES-175 Color Gallery, Chronology, Shipping Totals, and more. This book is a must for every guitar player and enthusiast or collector.

00001134 ....$24.95

THE GIBSON 335
Its History and Its Players

by Adrian Ingram

Gibson's first "semi-acoustic" the ES-335, which was neither totally solid nor fully acoustic, is the guitar of choice used by many famous guitarists such as Andy Summers, Elvin Bishop, Lee Ritenour, Jay Graydon, Robben Ford, Freddie King, John McLaughin, Jimmy Page, Chuck Berry, Tony Mottola, Johnny Rivers, Jack Wilkins, Bono, Grant Green, Eric Clapton, Stevie Ray Vaughan, Alvin Lee, B.B. King, Emily Remler, Otis Rush, Pete Townshend, John Lee Hooker, and Larry Carlton. This book includes the complete history of the 335, the players, a beautiful color section, chronology, shipping totals and more. A must-have for every 335 player and guitar enthusiast or collector!

00000353 120 pages........................$29.95

THE GIBSON L5

by Adrian Ingram

Introduced in 1922, the Gibson L5 is the precursor of the modern archtop guitar. This book takes a look at its history and most famous players, from its creation, through the Norlin years, to its standing today as the world's most popular jazz guitar. Includes a 16-page full color photo section.

00000216 112 pages........................$29.95

GRETSCH – THE GUITARS OF THE FRED GRETSCH COMPANY

by Jay Scott

This comprehensive manual uncovers the history of Gretsch guitars through 32 pages of color photos, hundreds of black & white photos, and forewords by Fred Gretsch, George Harrison, Randy Bachman, Brian Setzer, and Duane Eddy. It covers each model in depth, including patent numbers and drawings for collectors.

00000142 286 pages........................$35.00

THE HISTORY & ARTISTRY OF NATIONAL RESONATOR INSTRUMENTS

by Bob Brozman

This book is a history book, source book and owner's manual for players and fans that covers the facts and figures necessary for serious collectors. In addition to many black and white historical photos, there is a 32-page color section, and appendixes with serial numbers for all instruments, a company chronology, and a Hawaiian Artist Discography.

00000154 296 pages........................$35.00

P.O. Box 17878 - Anaheim Hills, CA 92817
(714) 779-9390   www.centerstream-usa.com